The Last White Parliament

The Last White Parliament

F Van Zyl Slabbert

Sidgwick & Jackson
London

First published in 1985 by
Hans Strydom Publishers
P O Box 29097
Melville 2109
Republic of South Africa
and
Jonathan Ball Publishers
P O Box 548
Bergvlei
2012 Johannesburg

This edition published by
Sidgwick & Jackson Limited
London

ISBN 283 99349 9

Contents

'Men fight and lose the battle and the thing they fought for comes about in spite of their defeat, and when it comes, turns out not to be what they meant and other men have to fight for what they meant under another name.'

William Norris
The Ballad of John Ball

Author's note

This is not a comprehensive historical account, although I hope it is historically accurate. It is a personal account in which anecdotes illustrate analyses of a period of my own life in which I experienced and participated in the changes which are interpreted in the following pages.

I dedicate this effort to my daughter, Tania, and son, Riko, with the wish that they may better understand me and the times in which I have been involved.

F Van Zyl Slabbert MP
February 1985

Acknowledgements

To Bob and Coral for the tranquillity of Boshimela. To my secretary, Jenny Nothard, more thanks than I can adequately convey for typing, patience and encouragement. Anna-Hilge Gagiano made it as readable as is humanly possible by checking grammar, syntax and breakdowns in elementary literacy. Again Dian Joubert demonstrated his unnerving feel for style and context and I remain the culprit for failing to do justice to either.

Finally, to the real politicians – voluntary workers on constituency executives and committee room clerks.

F Van Zyl Slabbert

1974: a stumble into politics

My mother died a few days after I accepted the nomination of the Progressive Party as their candidate in the 1974 General Election for the Cape Town constituency of Rondebosch. I was Professor of Sociology at the University of Witwatersrand at the time and when I returned from Cape Town I found a telegram on my desk at the University which read: 'The old girl died yesterday. What must I do?'

It was from my half-brother Sean (I call him Shamus). He was about 16 then and living alone with her. The last time I had seen her alive Shamus and I took her out to dinner when I was doing external examination work at Natal University in October of the previous year. It was a very good evening.

She died of alcoholism. For the last four days of life she was comatose with a grossly distended liver. Shamus and his girlfriend were alone with her during this time. That was why he sent me that telegram. As a sixteen-year-old he had no-one else to turn to. The practical problem of burying someone occupied my mind on the flight to Durban. And I thought of her.

My sister and I (we are twins) were taken away from her when we were seven years old, and since then she had made herself felt in our lives by her absence.

We were looked after by an aunt and uncle and grandparents until we finished high school, but like most children, we hoped that our divorced parents would somehow become reconciled. In retrospect it is quite clear that this was never possible, and also undesirable. My father is married to his third wife (a half sister having been produced by him and the second), and my mother married again – her husband died a few years before her – and they had been responsible for Shamus.

It would be untrue to say that I had an unhappy childhood. Although we practically lived in school hostels from the age of nine, we grew up in the rural Northern Transvaal, were very well looked after and loved by an aunt and uncle and our paternal grandparents (the maternal ones being dead), and we enjoyed school life. We were popular and very successful in terms of peergroup standards of achievement: head-boy, head-girl, first team captain of this and that, and so on.

I saw my mother infrequently. But, whenever I did, it left a vivid memory: rushing to her aid when my grandfather was throttling her in fierce anger over something I did not understand; taking her to a bioscope, looking at *The Alamo* with John Wayne (her favourite) for the third time and basking in her enthusiasm; her Sunday cooking. Even today, these and many other things make her alive in my mind. I never doubted her love for us, and yet I somehow sensed that she could not, or would not, tell me and my sister how to cope with life. This, looking back now, was the enigmatic part of her in my own emotional development. I knew my mother loved me but that I was essentially on my own when it came to facing up to whatever life presented. Early on it cultivated a sense of independence, a suspicion of blind authority and of automatic adult 'wisdom'. She was by far the most intelligent, exciting and original person in my young world, and in every conventional sense of the word she was a failure – as a mother, a wife, a worker, a neighbour, a socially responsible person. It did not lead me to dismiss convention, although I have always retained a strong scepticism of it. Early on, too, I developed a soft spot for the underdog, a tolerance for the outsider and the outcast.

The last time I saw her, I was shocked. Shamus opened the flat door and she was sitting in the stinkwood easy chair. She wore thick-rimmed glasses which magnified her eyes into a wide myopic stare; her face was blotched and her legs heavily swollen. I had come to take them to dinner after marking exam scripts for the last two days. I sensed that I would not see her again.

Usually, when we met on these infrequent occasions she would pretend control over the drinking and decline any offer I made in this respect. This time I told her that I insisted we enjoy ourselves for old times' sake. We had a good time. Later that night, pleasantly inebriated and supported on each side by Shamus and myself, we helped her up the stairs to the flat. I remember feeling very warm and kindly towards her. She pinched my neck when she hugged me goodbye.

The next I heard of her was Shamus's telegram. She was about fifty-three years old.

At the airport I was met by Stan Kahn, a friend and academic colleague, Shamus and his girlfriend. Stan offered me his car, took us to the flat and left us to get on with the funeral arrangements. The next morning, we went to the funeral parlour and negotiated a coffin and a funeral service. On Thursday noon a Roman Catholic priest was available to conduct a service. Shamus's father was a Roman Catholic. So it was not all that strange, although it would not have mattered one whit to her – alive or dead. We then saw a lawyer at SANTAM insurance who was to execute her will – a perfunctory duty as her debts outstripped her assets by a considerable margin – and he assured us that no claims could be made against any of her descendants, not that that would have made much difference to the problem either.

I had made it clear to Shamus that he was going back with me to my wife and children, so we had to close up the flat and dispense with its contents as soon as possible. I asked Stan Kahn to hold an informal auction amongst our University colleagues for the furniture, put whatever we valued into storage and finalize the lease on the flat. We were sitting in the flat, reasonably satisfied that we had dealt with the situation, when we started thinking about the procedure of burial itself. We did not have enough people to carry the coffin. It was only Shamus and myself. The funeral was twenty-four hours away. The funeral parlour said a minimum of six bearers could cope and if we were short they could provide some help. This was unacceptable. Shamus had some half-brothers from my mother's second husband's first marriage. Two were available – Stan Kahn was also there. I phoned my father, who also lived in the area and asked him if he was prepared to help. He made the sixth bearer.

I hero-worshipped my father for the first ten years of my life largely because his mother (my grandmother) presented him to me in larger than life dimensions. As children, we saw him even less frequently than our mother, so there was no way of testing her eulogies about him. He was the youngest child of six with an extremely authoritarian and intolerant father and a sweet and gentle mother. As soon as he could he rushed into blind rebellion and sowed his wild oats with a vengeance.

In the process he met my mother and found himself a reluctant husband and father-to-be by the age of twenty. This proved to be only a temporary hiccup in his rebellion against whatever ailed him. He left us when we were two years old. We saw each other at odd times.

The first time I really began to experience him as a person was when I was sixteen and he living with his third wife. By then he had succumbed to the pressures of convention without really knowing why and bore very little resemblance to my grandmother's loving recollections. I got to know him as a kindly man, lacking in self-confidence, apologetic to the point of irritation, overly sentimental and thriving on reminiscences of the past to cope with the pain and inadequacies of the present. A simple, inoffensive person. The difference between him and my mother was that he, inexplicably to himself, felt he had to apologize for whatever he had done, while she could never see the point of it all.

Driving around in Stan Kahn's tan coloured Volvo with Ceres registration, I began to notice sometimes one, sometimes two cars following us. I mentioned this to Stan and he apologized, saying that it was quite possibly the security police. He often visited a friend who was under house arrest at the time and the Volvo was under surveillance. It amused me to think that the security police were following me almost as if to make sure that my mother's funeral arrangements went off smoothly.

On the day of the funeral it was hot and humid as only Durban can be at that time of the year. We had to be at the cemetery gates at a quarter to twelve to meet the hearse. On the way we picked up an office colleague of my mother's whom I did not know. The security police were still following the car. They must have departed when the hearse arrived, because they were definitely not part of the procession which followed the hearse on foot to the grave-site. It was a long walk down a hill and the procession was about twenty-five strong including the personnel of the funeral parlour. Those whom I did not know, I was told, were colleagues or friends of my mother. When we got to the grave I could feel the sweat trickling down my back. We stopped and stood waiting for the priest to arrive. I cannot remember what he looked like and I have forgotten his name. We shook hands and he told us to carry the coffin to the grave. It was all over in five minutes. I thanked those present for being there and said a few words to the effect that my mother had always been a lonely person whom peace of mind had eluded and that I hoped she wasn't tortured any more.

Stan Kahn was the only one I noticed crying on one side. We shovelled sand in and dropped rose petals on the coffin. Childhood memories held me in silence. All of us walked back awkwardly to where the cars were parked and dispersed to our various points. We were back in her flat before one o'clock. I had sent Shamus's girlfriend back to Kimberley the previous day, so all we had to do was to finalize a few last-minute arrangements with Stan Kahn before he took us to the airport.

A week later I started campaigning in Cape Town for the April 1974 general election. I suppose nothing could have prepared me adequately for the world I was about to enter. I stumbled into it almost by accident. After teaching at four Universities in South Africa, I ended up as a Professor and Head of the Department of Sociology at the University of the Witwatersrand. Each time I moved, it was in the hope that I could find a better opportunity to become a competent academic. Wits was the fourth place where this hope had been frustrated. I inherited a bureaucratic and administrative mess; there were virtually no research funds and a senior colleague was riddled with complexes and problems. I enjoyed lecturing but did not have enough time to do research and read and had visions of becoming, at the age of thirty-three, a second-rate academic house-keeper for the rest of my life. I suppose I was ripe to consider alternatives.

In addition, my intellectual interests had moved away from general theory and philosophy to problems of change in developing or third world countries, particularly South and Southern Africa.

In fact, I was preparing a paper for a conference in Connecticut, USA, on 'Afrikaner Nationalism, White Politics and Change', when the general election was announced. Therefore I had a keen interest in political developments in my own country, although I had never belonged to or actively supported any political party. Generally speaking, I was not very interested in so-called white politics.

There was another factor which I cannot easily articulate. It had to do with the old dilemma in South Africa: the relationship between political awareness, morality and political action. This dilemma had reached and has maintained almost epidemic proportions amongst academics in South Africa. We debated with and abused each other endlessly about it. We competed with each other in defining the com-

5

plexity of the South African problem, engaged in moral outbidding in assessing the quality of each other's involvement or lack of it, or speculated on the timing and extent of the 'crunch'. The latter usually had to do with one's favourite theory of social change and the forces that would bring it about. I do not wish to belittle this dilemma. On the contrary, too much speculation on the relationship between the significance of individual political involvement and intellectual appreciation of what is actually needed to bring about the desired change, usually has a paralysing effect on a person's actions. This is why many of our able academics agonize about their inaction with stimulating and penetrating articles, papers and books on the problem. The fact that I became involved in the manner in which I did does not imply that I have resolved this dilemma successfully. I mention it to show that, at the time, I was ready to try something other than what I had been doing to cope with it.

This did not mean I was thinking of another career or disenchanted with being an academic. I can think of few more pleasant forms of sheltered employment in industrial society. However, I must have been in an amenable frame of mind when two United Party MPs approached me with a request that I run as a candidate in one of their safer seats in the Johannesburg area. I found the suggestion ludicrous. Not only because I found the participation of the United Party (then the official Opposition in Parliament) on a commission of inquiry into certain organizations and individuals – which led to the arbitrary persecution of some of my friends and people whom I admire – extremely offensive, but also because the possibility of becoming a Member of Parliament under the present circumstances in South Africa had never entered my mind. But these two gentlemen, Horace van Rensburg and Dick Enthoven, were very persistent.

They assured me that a group of Young Turks were intent on a take-over bid of the United Party, that it was going to alter its stance radically and force the pace of change.

'The time has come to do something rather than just analyse', they emphasized.

I never doubted their sincerity, only the tenability of their assumptions about what they could achieve. Eventually I said I would talk to my friend, Professor Nic Olivier, at Stellenbosch University and see if he was interested. Nic said he did not mind talking about it and that he would even fly up for the occasion. It was agreed that we would come together for a dinner at Horace van Rensburg's house.

That evening Horace, his wife, Japie Basson (a senior front bencher) and his wife, Hennie Serfontein (a Sunday Times political journalist), Nic and myself were present. We were joined later on by Dick Enthoven. The wine flowed freely and the tongues loosened apace. First they tried to persuade us both, but soon switched all the attention to Nic. I have to acknowledge that I helped to persuade Nic as well by emphasizing that if he had no moral objections it would be interesting to give it a go. He did not put up too much of a fight and finally succumbed. Nic then joined them in trying to persuade me. I protested my moral considerations and he countered by saying that we must go in and change all that and asked why I was trying to persuade him to do something I was not prepared to do. And so it went.

In the early hours of the morning a spirit of solidarity and determination prevailed to collapse all unnecessary contradictions immediately. Major political obstacles had been reduced to irresistible challenges and we were ready to break down the front door and go and look for the enemy. Horace with a squint in his eyes typical of too much wine and too little sleep, assured me that he wanted no final commitment from either of us. All he wanted was for Nic and myself to sign membership cards and say that we would consider standing 'in principle'.

We still had to be approved by the candidates' committee of the United Party before anything could be finalized, he explained. I had a moment of lucidity whilst completing the membership card and quietly slipped it into my pocket. When I took Nic back to his hotel I told him about this and said there was no way I could go through with it. He was disappointed and said the time would come when I would also have to pay my pound of flesh. Horace and his wife apparently spent until dawn, eventually on all fours, looking for my membership card. It was a long time before his wife spoke to me again.

The Sunday Times the next morning had Nic and me on the front page as potential candidates and signed up members of the United Party. Other newspapers, friends and even a few strangers phoned to verify and I denied the story. Among them was Jan van Eck who worked for the Progressive Party. He said that Colin Eglin, the Leader, was coming up to Johannesburg and would like to see me. I made it quite clear that I wasn't interested in standing, but said that I was quite happy to talk to Eglin. My role in persuading Nic bothered me. I felt guilty.

Eglin said that 1974 was a make or break election for the Progressive Party. For thirteen years Helen Suzman had been the only member and this time they hoped to get another seat or else pack it in. The extra one they hoped for was his own in Sea Point, but they needed to keep the United Party busy in a few adjoining ones. He wanted me to stand in Rondebosch and assured me that it was very unlikely that I could win and that the vote was 3–1 against the Progressive Party. The fact that I could not win was a definite attraction in standing. I thought it would be an interesting experience and in some way I felt I would be fulfilling my obligation to Nic Olivier.

And so I became a candidate – confident that I would be back at the University after 24 April, the day of the election. After almost signing a membership card for the United Party, I was now fighting them. I found the latter prospect much more satisfying then the former though I had some difficulty with the image and aspects of the policy of the Progressive Party. I fully supported their stand on civil liberties and this, I suppose, made it easier on my conscience to stand. I joined the PP on the day I officially accepted nomination.

From Monday to Friday I lectured in Johannesburg and from Friday to Sunday I campaigned in Cape Town. This went on for about seven weeks. It was like trying to reconcile the irreconcilable. I was oscillating between the aloof, private and slightly bohemian world of Academia and the involved, public and very conventional world of politics. I thought initially the only escape was detachment, distancing myself from myself as if watching something happening to someone else. But I had not reckoned with the response of people and the earnestness of their involvement. The campaign appeared to be a life and death matter to them. By the end of seven weeks there were almost 200 of them working nonstop and crowding the campaign office. The public in the constituency were fired up with enthusiasm. This was middle to upper class English-speaking South Africa beginning to question the relevance of their own traditional establishment. Since 1948 the United Party had been part of their political world like gin and tonic on Sunday before lunch. This was precisely why I was so confident I could not win. And yet, halfway through, a campaign that was regarded as hopeless became hopeful. Exactly why I do not know. The fact that I was Afrikaans and from Stellenbosch obviously helped. This combination, particularly when it was opposed to Government, had an almost mystical appeal to English-speaking voters in those days. I was eulogized as some seven-day charismatic wonder that could swing the dog by the tail.

At house meetings I was introduced as a new young Smuts and grey-haired ladies were weepy and misty-eyed. It was ridiculous, but there was nothing to be done about it. The campaign had gathered its own momentum. The extraordinary thing was that halfway through I wanted to win. For the life of me I could not think what the political significance of such a victory was going to be, nor what I was going to do as a Member of Parliament. I suppose it was because nobody gave it a chance from the start; because it was such obvious fun to disrupt the establishment, to confuse the bridge parties, knitting circles, book clubs and cake sales with new options; because so many people worked so hard for so many reasons; because and because and because. Although I was the glamour boy of the campaign the real and backbreaking campaign work was done by people like John Whitehead, Marie Levitan and Neill Ross.

I worked myself to a standstill. Not for the first time, but definitely again, I neglected all else, wife and family included, to feed the fire in my belly. (This total immersion in something eventually contributed in no small measure to the breakup of my marriage). Those last days of the campaign were pure frenzy. I had been talking, shaking hands, writing statements, addressing house meetings, fielding voters from the pavements, meeting opinion leaders, placating prima donnas, lunching journalists and editors almost non-stop for six, seven weeks. Yet almost every night I would end up alone either in a flat or guest room somewhere in the constituency. I suppose fatigue precluded an objective awareness of what was happening to me. Everything in me resisted the kind of life I was heading for. The loss of anonymity, the false confidence of public speaking, the boring conventionality, the intellectual dullness of pub-talk politics, the obligatory ritual of public life. I was off my mind to let myself get trapped into it. Yet, the next morning, I was into the day's appointments and demands as if it were all that mattered.

I remember having a swimming pool all to myself on a hot afternoon, at one of the wealthy homes in Bishopscourt. I had run into Jonathan Wacks, a colleague and very close friend, and asked him to join me.

He is extremely intelligent and perceptive, with a well-developed sense of the absurd, and he just could not see me as a politician in white politics and the more he explained why, the more I had to agree with him. And yet, we both knew that the chances were improving daily of my becoming one. I said to him that the only thing I really found attractive about it was that I would be coming back to Cape Town.

As I tried to make clear, there was no sense of destiny calling, a desire to save the nation or any other such lofty political motivation which led me into public office. I was not attracted to the life style or such perks as I was aware of at the time. A combination of factors interlocked to propel me towards a decision based on reasonable assumptions that turned out to be false. And so I found myself with Mana, my former wife, at 3 am, 24 April 1974 on the roof of a Volkswagen Combi outside the Magisterial Courts of Wynberg, surrounded by screaming, cheering and crying people. I had just been proclaimed the Member of Parliament for Rondebosch. I responded to their elation and waved and laughed, but at the same time kept asking myself 'Sweet suffering grace, what am I going to do now?'

'How come you, an Afrikaner ...?'

One question which never failed to crop up: 'But you, an Afrikaner, how is it possible you think the way you do?' It is asked by Afrikaans and English speakers; foreigners, as well as South Africans. There is, of course, one level of posing this question which does not really deserve to be taken seriously. This is the level of the stereotype, of conventional wisdom about the characteristics of Afrikaners (or Jews, or English for that matter). For example I had impeccable credentials in terms of which non-Afrikaners could typecast me as typical, or fellow Afrikaners could infer that I could make it to the top within the Afrikaner establishment. I came from the conservative rural Northern Transvaal, studied Theology for four and a half years at Stellenbosch before beginning to lecture there, played rugby for Stellenbosch, South African Universities and so on. In other words, the question has a one-dimensional significance in the sense that, given all the established criteria in terms of which (if I conformed) I could not fail to be a success: why did I choose not to become one? I do not know, and I have never been interested in finding out. This sort of thing: non-conformity, deviance, rejecting the establishment, happens all over the world and psychologists pre-occupy themselves with identifying the factors which shape the individual psyche towards this kind of attitude.

Even if they have the answer, and I doubt they do, my reaction would still be: so what? It will not help me to understand my society and myself in relation to it. To pose the question in this way is to remove me from the history of my country.

The level at which the question deserves to be taken more seriously is also the level on which it is more difficult to answer. What were the factors in my experience which I can pin-point as shaping my own awareness? Why do I think the way I do about races, people, politics, power, my country? There is a much more complex and multi-dimensional level of coming to grips with the question. Being the Afrikaner

I am is far more interesting and problematical than being the Afrikaner others expect me to be. And in trying to answer the question the dangers of distortion, of oversimplification, self-aggrandizement, retrospective cleverness, historical 'neatness' are always present. Good analysis is always a brief respite against randomness. In self-analysis, the temptation to present myself as the first cause should be resisted, otherwise it loses credibility. On the other hand, too much modesty is equally boring and unconvincing. I have to accept that when people ask me questions of this kind, I am important or puzzling enough for them to want to hear the answer. I can only try.

Throughout my life, but particularly in my formative years, my experience with black people has had a real influence on my own thinking. The disparity between my personal experience of them and the 'official' or generalized white view introduced a tension within me that had to be constantly confronted. Much later on I was struck by the fact that in the political philosophy of different parties and movements the concept black was an abstraction, a series of definitions and assumptions, rather than a reference to any living person I had met or experienced.

My first clear recollection in this regard is of Florina. This was before we, my sister and I, were taken away from my mother, before our seventh year. We lived in Duncan Street, Brooklyn, Pretoria, in a huge rambling house. To a large extent we were neglected, roaming around with a neighbourhood gang of much older children and I remember walking long distances underground in storm water drains, stealing fruit and sweets from cafés and shops and jostling for position in the pecking order of our group. But at night we were alone in the house, except for Florina, whose bedroom was in the garage. I would lie watching the shadows of the poinsettia leaves weaving and waving on the wall, reflected from the street light outside.

I was much more terrified of the dark and the loneliness of night than my sister and I used to strain my ears for a car that would slow down and enter our driveway signalling my mother's return. Eventually, creaking with fright, I would suggest to my sister that we go and lie with Florina. She was larger than life-size: enormous buttocks and stomach with two medium-sized watermelons for bosoms and shiny round cheeks. Her bed was raised on bricks at all four corners to keep away the Tokoloshi (an evil spirit in the shape of a dwarf) and was behind a makeshift curtain which she used to split the garage into different rooms. Once she had drawn that curtain and we had snuggled in behind her ample frame it was like bedding down in a bomb shelter of security. Florina's comfort and love predisposed me kindly and instinctively towards black mammas for the rest of my life.

Years later, when I was already an MP and accepting the honour of becoming a patron of the Mother City Football Club in Langa, at a party in one of the community halls in the township, one of the mammas wriggled and shuffled towards me on the rhythm of some African music and smiled and chuckled me into dancing with her. It was Florina all over again.

William Dini taught me about nature and how to live on a farm. I was nine and we were living with our grandparents on a farm called Turffontein. We attended a farm school known as Marabastad Laer Skool and went home every weekend.

I used to live for those weekends. William Dini was about four years older than I was and already working as a labourer. Weekends he was free and during school holidays I would work with him occasionally, or sometimes try and get him off to come and play. My grandfather, for a number of reasons (one of them being that I was the third generation bearer of his name), suspended his intolerance and authoritarianism when it came to me (much to the enduring chagrin of my sister) and showered me with affection and favouritism.

We played barefoot soccer with a tennis ball (he had feet like concrete blocks) swam in the mud dam and hunted hare and guinea fowl with knobkerries. He taught me how to lead oxen while his father ploughed. We were both terrified of Abel Dini who could hold the plough with one hand and crack the whip behind your right ear if you did not lead in a straight line. William Dini was the first person I saw masturbating and I remember flushing hot with confusion when he fondled the young maidens in the field. He would laugh deep down from the back of his throat. He took me to Mapela's Kraal for a stokvel (party) where I drank sorghum beer and watched the grown men fight amongst themselves. Now, in retrospect, I recognize him as one of those irrepressible, spontaneous, inquiring spirits that have always attracted me.

I remember the awkwardness that entered our relationship, when, after we had moved to town and I was already in High School, he became the cook in the house. My grandfather's brutal paternalism towards him grated me. Many times I watched William Dini clench his teeth and look into the distance. One day he told me he could never settle for this kind of life; that he was going to Johannesburg to be his own boss. Somehow he managed to be employed by my aunt and uncle in Johannesburg, but when I visited there the next school holiday, he was gone.

One evening after church a group of us were walking back to the hostel when one of them asked, 'Would you like to come with us and have some fun?' I was two years away from matriculation; he was slightly my senior, and as two of my best friends had already said yes, I went along. It was very flattering for the most senior boys to ask us younger ones to go and do secret things with them. There was a nine pm curfew for blacks in Pietersburg. A long mournful hooter would sound to warn that all blacks had to be out of the white part of town. The fun was to find any black who had missed the curfew and beat him up. The first I knew of this was when I saw a black man pedalling furiously on his bicycle and two of our group jumped out and pushed him off balance. When he fell, they rushed in to kick and punch him. I shouted and tried to stop them, but they laughed and pushed me aside. I saw the black man bleeding from the mouth and pleading for mercy and I ran away retching and coughing with nausea. I remember thinking that he had not harmed any of us; that it could have been anybody and they would have beaten him up, as long as he was black. I could not believe that this was going on without anybody doing something to prevent it.

Shortly after this incident I had a religious conversion and became very involved with the Students' Christian Association. This no doubt helped me to start a crusade against this kind of 'fun', and although I was initially branded as a *kaffir-boetie* (nigger lover), the campaign was successful and that brand of senseless brutality stopped.

My religious involvement also found an outlet in missionary activity and every Sunday afternoon for the last two years of school I went to the black male wards of the local hospital and tried to tell the patients more about Christianity and the Christian way of life. Most of them were simple peasant folk who were beginning to experience the dislocation and vagaries of migrant life. It was like talking to a brick wall. I remember those sweltering afternoons, flies buzzing, patients lying on and under beds and me trying to convey the blessings awaiting them if only they would believe. I desperately wanted them to be helped.

One early evening, when I was a first-year student at Witwatersrand University and staying with the aunt and uncle that William Dini had worked for before he disappeared, he suddenly reappeared, full of bravado, strutting and boasting that he was now his own man. He told me that in a short while he would show me that he had his own car. I asked him how he would get it and what he was doing at present. He laughed his old laugh and playfully punched me in the stomach. It was clear that he was a member of a township gang. We promised to keep in touch, but I have never seen him since that day.

It was 1959 and Wits University had a Fellowship Society that ran lunch-hour meetings on the South African political situation. For a well-meaning, overly devout rugby playing farm boy who had never given an analytical thought to politics, these meetings were traumatic in their impact.

The first one I attended was addressed by Robert Sobukwe, who was tutor/lecturer at the University and leader of the Pan African Congress. The organization was later banned and Sobukwe jailed on Robben Island for nine years. He was late for the meeting and in apologizing for this explained that he had been stopped by a young policeman who demanded his reference book (pass).

On seeing that it was in order, he dropped it to the ground, put his foot on it and told Sobukwe to pick it up. As Sobukwe related this incident, an angry buzz rose from the black members of the audience who were sitting in one large block comprising about half of an audience of 500–600. Sobukwe made an impassioned speech demanding black participation in Government and when, during question time, one white student quietly and almost timidly asked him whether he thought blacks were ready to govern a complex industrial society, the black block of the audience jumped out of their seats as if electrically shocked and shouted in one voice, 'Right now!'

A week later, M C Botha, Minister of Bantu Administration (black affairs) addressed the same fellowship society and when told about the reference book incident experienced by Sobukwe, smugly and with a defiant smile, as if he anticipated the question, took out his own white reference book (ID book) and explained that he was also compelled to carry one. One year later Sobukwe led a Pan African Congress defiance campaign against the 'pass' system which ended in a pass-burning ceremony and the Sharpeville shootings that reverberated right around the world.

I was then a second-year student at Stellenbosch University studying for a BA degree that would allow me to do Theology at the Seminary of the University.

One Sunday morning a group of about ten of us (most of them aspiring Dutch Reformed dominees at the Seminary and much my seniors as students) left with the Professor of Missionary Science to go and preach in Langa. I had seen a picture earlier in the week in the local newspaper showing a nurse with blood running down her face from a cut caused by the stoning of her car's wind-screen. So politically naïve were we that this did not alert us to the mood prevailing in the townships at the time. We split into groups of two and walked into the township to find a convenient spot from which to deliver our message. My senior stopped at a tin shanty and started conversing with the inhabitants. It soon became obvious to me that he was more involved in defending the policy of separate development or apartheid than spreading the Gospel. Very soon we were surrounded by a group that steadily grew in number. I noticed the odd stone being thrown in our direction and the crowd becoming increasingly agitated. So impassioned was my senior in his talk that he was oblivious to the increasing hostility. I tugged him by his sleeve and told him we had better move out. He paled when it dawned on him what was happening and we began to walk into the crowd towards the exit.

They shouted insults and pushed and tripped us. Now and then a small stone would hit me on the shoulder or the head. It was a long walk back to the car. From the corner of my eye I saw the sixty-year-old Professor being frog-marched out of a side street to the exit. When we reached the car we hurriedly got in and tried to move away, but the crowd started rocking the car and moving its back end into some loose sand. The wheels churned up sand and dust while they laughed and spat on the windows. Four of us had to get out and push. I remember sand covering our sweaty faces as we shoved and heaved. Eventually we got away and we drove back to Stellenbosch in silence. I never did missionary work again – at least of a religious kind.

About six years later Dr Piet Koornhof, Deputy Minister at the time, came to Stellenbosch one evening to address a gathering of academics at a private house meeting. I was already lecturing in Sociology. A life-long friend, Rocky (Jannie) Gagiano, who lectured in Political Science, was also at the meeting. Koornhof was giving us an insight into the blacks of Soweto – their aspirations and frustrations – as reported in some confidential survey conducted for the Government at their request.

Rocky and I listened in disbelief at the picture that was presented to us. The gist of it was that political considerations were very low on the list of priorities for the average Sowetan and that their major concern was with their material welfare. We were astounded that Koornhof apparently could not see the link between politics and problems of material welfare. I had to attend my sister's wedding in Johannesburg soon after, so I suggested to Rocky that he and I try and arrange a gathering in a house in Soweto, present ourselves as young Afrikaner academics and repeat Koornhof's presentation to see what the reaction would be. We were a bit afraid of the possibility of violence, but found the idea very exciting. I contacted M T Moerane, then Editor of the *World* (a paper subsequently banned), and someone whom I came to know quite well, asking him to assist. He was more than willing. Thus we found ourselves early one evening at M T's house having a drink and a quick bite to eat before going to another house in Dube for the meeting.

While we were eating a man came in and M T introduced him as the only black dentist in South Africa. He was slightly drunk and appeared to be playfully belligerent. He kept asking rhetorical but aggressive questions.

'Why do you come and disturb us in our misery? Do you think we are animals in a zoo to be looked at?'

I kept saying he should come to the meeting and hear why we were there. Eventually he leaned towards me, lightly punching me in the stomach, and said he could not afford to go to the meeting as there were no street lights in front of his house and his wife had been raped the previous week.

The house in Dube was middle class by any standards and luxurious by Soweto's. There were about 70 people crowded into a fairly large living room – teachers, journalists, nurses, business men and some artists – the shakers and movers of the local scene. Moerane was blunt to the point of shock in his introduction. We were made to sit in the one corner on two little riempie chairs and Moerane simply said: 'Good evening Ladies and Gentlemen, these are two young Afrikaner academics from Stellenbosch and they wish to talk to you.' The silence rolled over us and I pitched in, repeating Koornhof's story.

I spoke for twenty minutes. For the next two-and-a-half hours Rocky and I did not, or rather could not, even if we wanted to, say a word.

We experienced abuse, threats, hysterical anger and inarticulate frustration. It washed over us, wave after wave. Eventually a voice spoke from the back saying we must go back to where we came from; that the blacks were very happy. All they wanted was to go to their homelands, but they wanted guns, lots of them, so that while their women and children were dying behind them they could go over the border and kill every white in sight. It was the dentist. He had come to the meeting after all. We then explained what the real purpose of our coming to Soweto was: that we were not Nationalists; that we rejected apartheid and separate development; that we were trying to get to know the real South Africa a little better; that we had no grand solutions. Moerane backed us up in a most eloquent and flattering fashion. There was a stunned silence initially; we were expecting more anger, when someone started chuckling and more and more started laughing. A young photographer came up to me and slapped me on the shoulder, hugged me and said, 'That was cool man, real cool.'

In retrospect it is clear that a jangle of emotions had been released. The satisfaction of having reached us who were intimately connected with power to tell us how they felt; the surprise and pleasure that young Afrikaners from Stellenbosch had done what we had done and the need to show that they were not totally bitter and twisted and could let their hair down.

By two-thirty am drinks were still being forced on us and they pleaded with us to stay. We drove to where we were staying and I remember struggling with a sense of futility and feeling depressed.

I suppose it would be impossible for any white to give an adequate account of how he or she developed political awareness in South Africa without reflecting on his or her interaction with blacks. From

Government policy (and more often than not because of it), down to the most intimate daily ritual, this aspect pervades our lives. Particularly if we are white. Blacks on the average know far better how whites live than the other way round. In my anecdotal accounts of my experience with blacks the danger of distortion is always at hand. What I have tried to show is that I experienced them as 'real' people: their love, friendship, hostility, anger, even rejection and remoteness. In South African white political life these people become abstractions; they function as political definitions in policy statements. Collective desires and characteristics are ascribed to them which say more about the fears and prejudices of those who believe in these policies than is true of any blacks I have come across; whether tribal or urban.

Of course black people are capable of reacting exactly the same way to whites, and some certainly do. This forms a large component of white fear of black response to oppression and deprivation. But that is another matter.

The growth of whatever awareness I now have did not depend only on my interaction with blacks. Sport played an important role as well. I loved to watch and participate in it. Any kind – even today I am a sucker for competition or a contest. Two things were important – the nature of the challenge and the physical exertion involved. I am moved by athletic prowess and any kind of sporting achievement. Few things can be more stark, and compelling than the contest between a person and a stop-watch. It has a universal language which instantly makes the point. It is given to few to appreciate and understand how the atom is split, but the most universally common form of human excellence is sporting achievement. It allows us to marvel at one another across boundaries, races, culture and ideologies and makes us feel we have something to talk about.

We can instinctively appreciate it when someone has confronted adversity with success and taken on all odds – political, social, personal – and come out on top. Of course sport can be escapist (I have escaped unashamedly many times); it can become embroiled in political and exploitative practices. But whatever the circumstances, individual or team excellence has its own unique significance.

For white South Africans generally, sport is much more than this. It is more than a religion, it is a total strategy against a total onslaught; it is the guardian of our national character; the barometer of our despair or hope. It too often becomes ridiculous and silly. Particularly in the case of rugby. During my own development, rugby was still seen by Afrikaners as their statement on the British Empire; their way of bringing the English in South Africa down a peg or two. The battle between English and Afrikaans schools was always more fierce than between schools of the same 'tribe'. It was our way of coping with a perceived sense of social and cultural inferiority as well as of achieving excellence.

This was the prevailing mood towards rugby when I began devoting myself to it with unrestrained enthusiasm. The recognition it brought me at school gave me confidence and a sense of acceptance that for a time was more important than the enjoyment I derived from taking part. Being first team Captain and considered a very good loose forward obliterated any discomfort about not having had a normal family life or having parents who might be regarded as being socially awkward. What is more, I enjoyed the game.

As a student at Stellenbosch, and later, when teaching there, I began to question the role of rugby in my life. Ironically in the year I was beginning to enjoy the most recognition and playing the best rugby of my career, I began to lose interest in the game. It was 1962, I was twenty-two years old, studying BD at the Theological Seminary and BA Honours in Sociology. I began to take my studies more seriously too. I was increasingly alienated from the sub-culture surrounding the game as well as the time it demanded of me when I felt there were other more important things to do. First team rugby at Stellenbosch involves four afternoons a week apart from the game on Saturday.

But it was the sub-culture which most disillusioned me; the post mortems after the game with pot-bellied, beer-drinking 'experts' from way back; the sight of players continually ingratiating themselves with sporting correspondents for some coverage; the pseudo-patriotic ethos that pervaded discussions on the importance of rugby in our national life; seeing successful farmers grovelling at the feet of arrogant second year students simply because we were 'Maties' on tour in their vicinity. Mentally it was not only escapist, it was a social narcotic to anything else going on in our society. The same may be said of other club and national sports here and in other countries. It was through rugby I learnt that I did not like this aspect of organized sport. I did not discover this overnight. In fact I left Stellenbosch rugby and joined the town club, stocked mainly with farmers and working people from town. It may sound sacrilegious to some, but I enjoyed my rugby more at Van Der Stel Rugby Club than at Stellenbosch.

I captained Van Der Stel for a while, became Chairman of the Club and coached various university teams. Gradually, however, I withdrew from involvement in organized sport. It held no satisfaction for me and it prevented me from enjoying physical exertion for myself. Now I am more interested in jogging, swimming and the occasional game of squash.

But through rugby I came to know the average white South African; to mix comfortably and easily with him. Whenever I became too enthusiastic about a new theory on social and political change, I would think of a rugby party or a change room before a game and it would reduce the theory to less pretentious dimensions. To picture Van Der Stel Rugby Club with the members that I knew and whose company I enjoyed, in a truly non-racial South Africa, and also to visualize the accompanying changes in social and economic infrastructure as well as the supporting and funding institutions for a sporting club; but above all, to think that, for this to come about relatively peacefully, it was going to depend on the volition of the majority of white South Africans, was an awesome perspective on the enormity of the challenges that awaited us.

And yet, the worlds of Langa on a Sunday morning and the Van Der Stel Rugby Club on a Saturday night are inextricably bound up with one another. I remember the time when 'Fifty', one of those inevitable stalwarts of the club, got into difficulties with the disciplinary committee. I was chairman of the club at the time and automatically chairman of the disciplinary committee, and Fifty and I had become friends. He worked as a butcher for the local OK Bazaars and lived for the club, coaching the lowest team, helping with every club function and generally making himself indispensable when all the odd and unpleasant jobs cropped up. His problem was that he became belligerent when under the influence and one evening he got involved in an argument with Anthony, the Coloured barman in the club, punched him and spat on him. He was seen doing this by another club member who confirmed this informally to other club members. Appearing before the disciplinary committee Fifty denied that he had spat on Anthony or punched him. Instead he claimed that Anthony had insulted him. The member who saw this refused to give evidence stating that he was not prepared to give evidence against Fifty in favour of a Coloured. Anthony stated his version of the incident in a calm and dispassionate manner with a great deal of credibility. In camera I put it to the Committee that the circumstantial evidence was overwhelmingly in favour of Anthony's account and that unfortunately I had to confront Fifty with the fact that he had lied. My recommendation was that Fifty be expelled unconditionally from the club unless he was prepared to apologize to Anthony. When I put this to Fifty in front of the Committee he ranted that I was prepared to accept the word of a 'Hotnot'* above that of a white man and stormed out of the room.

He was expelled and three months later apologized and was accepted back into the Club. He could not survive without the Club.

Soon after this I left Stellenbosch to go and teach at the University of Cape Town and although I have maintained infrequent contact with Van Der Stel Rugby Club, I have withdrawn completely from organized club sport.

Another thread of experience which influenced the growth of my political awareness, was my religious involvement which stimulated an intellectual and spiritual inquiry that has endured. What started as a psychological need for acceptance and certainty, turned into a quest for truth and a concern with ethical problems. During the last two years of high school I was very much involved with religious activities. This involvement was precipitated by the conversion experience at a Student Christian Association holiday camp which I explained earlier. I was invited there by Oom Dries Steyn whose life task it was to go round to schools and organize activities for the Association. In retrospect, it is quite clear that the conversion experience was a culmination of a very deep need for emotional security and the desire to be accepted and absolved for my shortcomings.

The enthusiastic and unconditional promise of this at the camp, subsequently confirmed by other Christians wherever I went, created a sense of well-being and blessèdness in me. Before I finished school I

* Hottentot.

had read the Bible from cover to cover twice; held weekly and highly successful and popular prayer meetings; been to church twice every Sunday and I had done missionary work on Sunday afternoons. I had intended studying medicine but became so involved that after numerous discussions with Church leaders, including Beyers Naudé and Ben Marais, I decided that I was called to become a Dominee of the Nederduits Gereformeerde (Dutch Reformed) Church. This caused dismay in my family, none of whom were religious in a conventional sense. Their apprehension strengthened my resolve and I found myself studying Latin and Greek at Wits University in my first year in 1959. Wits was chosen for financial considerations (I could live in with my aunt and uncle) and partly for political reasons (my aunt hoped that somehow it would postpone the evil day when I would be swept into Nationalist Party politics; today she is a confirmed and fervent Nationalist). Because Wits did not have classical Hebrew, which I needed in order to graduate for the Divinity School, I went to Stellenbosch from my second year on. I chose Stellenbosch because of my infatuation with rugby. It was also a 'Springbok factory'.

I had already completed the required BA admission and was in the Divinity School when it became clear to me that I could not become a dominee. It would be neat and comfortable to say that my disenchantment flowed from the Dutch Reformed Church's involvement with the governing National Party and the practice of racism in the church. This was not so, although I was becoming increasingly aware and disturbed about it. My disillusionment was an intellectual and philosophical one. I no longer accepted what they were teaching me. It serves no purpose to go into the finer theological arguments. All I know is that the dogma I was being taught undermined what little faith I had and insulted my reason. Above all, it bore little relation to the world I was living in or the problems I was struggling with. I tried to talk to the Professors and even engaged them on some of the issues – particularly on the theology of Karl Barth, whom they regarded as a heretic and whom I liked. Their adverse reaction increased my tension. In my fifth year at University I realized that I was not going to carry on with what I had set out to do. I had borrowed money to study and worked as a disinfecting officer for the Johannesburg Municipality every long vacation to make some more.

My choice of career hung in the air. I was working on an MA in Sociology and for the time being would carry on with that, but I was determined not to go into the church. So one afternoon found me pedalling uphill into a furious South-easter on a borrowed bicycle whose chain slipped the cog once every cycle, thinking of how to explain to the Dean of Divinity at his home why I was not carrying on. I was reviewing the ponderous theological and philosophical chestnuts I would put forward and had visions of debating until the early hours of the morning, when the answer presented itself in all its simplicity. I did not want to argue, I wanted to get out. If God called me, then He could uncall me. I walked into the Dean's study, sat down and told him that I no longer felt called by God to become a dominee – in fact I could say it with more certainty and conviction than when I initially believed He had called me. The Dean coughed and shifted and tried to steer the discussion in the direction of a theological debate, but I stuck to my explanation. It was all over in ten minutes. We knelt and the Dean asked the Almighty to spare me for a job in the teaching profession (why I do not know) and also to care for my spiritual well-being. The sense of elation and freedom I experienced, racing down the hill on the old bicycle with the wind behind my back, remains one of the sweeter memories of my life.

The decision to leave Divinity School was an emotional and intellectual turning point in my life. I was becoming more and more irritated and frustrated with the world of organized religion; the overwhelming awareness of establishment and conformity; the whole network of sanctions that had permeated my thoughts and actions. But, more important, I felt dishonest about the way I was expected to think and believe. My friendship with Rocky Gagiano played a crucial role at this time. He was totally wrapped up in philosophy and I was beginning to discover social theory. Rocky was uncompromising in his pursuit of 'meaning' almost to the point of self-destruction. It was the early sixties and the prevailing mood in philosophy and social science in Europe and the United States of America concerned itself with existenialism, phenomenology and variations of psychoanalysis or *verstehen* sociology. It was considered desperately important to come to grips with problems of self-identity, alienation and the meaning of existence. It was also acceptable to be stupid and silly as long as you were 'totally honest' about it. Needless to say it led to a great deal of moral and intellectual self-indulgence. But it made me aware of my own motives and the sincerity of my convictions. My marathon sessions with Rocky on religion, morality and social obligation not only influenced my eventual decision to leave the Divinity School, but started a close and lasting friendship which thrives more than twenty years later.

Soon after this decision, I was offered a temporary junior lectureship in the Department of Sociology. I was launched into an academic career that lasted until I went into politics ten years later. The different phases of intellectual involvement were reflected in my personal and social life. I was never able to treat academic life as a nine-to-five career or to regard intellectual truth to be of no consequence to my personal life. I have not always been able to keep a consistent relationship between my intellectual and personal life – that would have been too unkind and even unnecessary to myself and many others – but I have never been able to separate the two from each other. Each one of us has his individual way of coping with what he knows, wants and has to do.

So after I left Theology and started teaching Sociology my first phase of intellectual interest was existentialist philosophy and *verstehen* sociology. This corresponded with a personal questioning of the establishment and conventional terms, a preoccupation with my own individuality and a questioning of group pressure and ideological dogmatism.

Rocky and I used to walk the streets of Cape Town right through the night, visiting night clubs and shebeens, talking to prostitutes, pimps, tramps, pushers and generally romanticizing the marginal people of society. Everything was so irrelevant and yet so agonizingly 'real'. More than one sunrise found us on a train to Stellenbosch or sitting at the docks of Table Bay reflecting on the uniqueness of life and the insult and inevitability of death. The sombreness of our thoughts was often compounded by our futile pursuit of promiscuous sexual relief and a throbbing hangover.

But I suppose I became bored eventually with seeing myself as the centre of the universe of meaning. You can only indulge in such excessive subjectivism for so long, unless you have pathological tendencies. In the sixties it became so common to be different that everyone ended up being the same. Protest and non-conformity had been successfully commercialized in song, dress and sub-cultures, and cult figures like Baez, Dylan, Marcuse and McCluhan soon became the establishment figures for a new generation to discredit. Intellectually my interest shifted from the subjective and concrete to the objective and abstract. Instead of trying to understand the exceptional and arbitrary I searched for laws and regularity.

I immersed myself in social theory and the philosophy of science. Much of what I read was beyond my comprehension but this increased my determination to understand as much as I could.

On the personal side this phase corresponded with the writing of my PhD thesis, getting married and seeing my daughter being born. I settled down to domestic life and made an earnest attempt to become an academic. My intellectual interest shifted again after I had completed my doctorate on a topic that was so esoteric in the South African social science context as to make intelligible conversation impossible with all but a handful of colleagues. In any case, despite my interest in it, I found it almost impossible to teach to students because of its interdisciplinary nature. I felt it more useful to apply some of the insights I had gained to a better understanding of South African and African society. And so it happened that I came into conflict, both intellectually and practically, with the policy of apartheid and/or separate development. I attended symposia, gave public talks and arranged meetings in order to expose the ideology and the policies that resulted from it. The more I became involved the more repugnant and offensive I found the Government's policy. Much has been written about it, its contradictions, immorality and conflict potential. I have tried to write about it myself.

The reason for my growing anger with it was and is with what it does to the interaction between human beings. It dehumanizes those who suffer from its disadvantages and brutalizes the humanity of those who enjoy its privileges.

I became more outspoken, both in my teaching and in my social life, against the policy. This appeared to create concern among some within the University establishment. I remember coming home one afternoon from coaching the rugby team of the residence of which I was the warden, when Mana, my former wife, told me that Oom Kosie Gericke, Moderator of the Dutch Reformed Church, local student preacher and member of the University Council, had called to inform me that I had been appointed deacon of the Student Church. I

26

was incredulous. Not only had I not been to church regularly for the last few years, but it should by then have been quite clear how I felt about the relationship between organized religion, politics and racism in South Africa. I went to see Oom Kosie, and explained that it was not possible for me to accept the appointment. He told me earnestly that I should think very carefully, that it was a crucial decision and if I accepted 'many doors would open' for my future career. I declined. It was 1968 and in retrospect that decision must have started my rejection by the Afrikaner Nationalist establishment.

I taught at Rhodes University for a year in 1969, but returned to Stellenbosch at the end of it, and by then my ostracism was quite noticeable. Ironically, it was Rocky Gagiano who brought this point home to me most forcibly. He had graduated and gone to Bonn, West Germany, for post-graduate study in philosophy. On his return he worked as a journalist for one of the daily newspaper groups and then began teaching Political Science at Stellenbosch. He had been back at Stellenbosch for a few months when he came to me one day and told me that he had been approached by an agent of the security police to find out whether he would convey information to them about some lecturers on the Stellenbosch University staff. Rocky mentioned three names: Degenaar, André du Toit and myself. We had a chuckle about this, but I realized that I was no longer viewed simply as an errant son, but as a potential enemy of the State – incredible dictum!

I again, and finally, left Stellenbosch for Cape Town University and the last phase of my intellectual career began before I found myself in white politics. The year was 1972 and there was a great deal of student political activity. Protest meetings and demonstrations were held against Government policy and much of the lively academic debate was taken up by discussions of strategies for, and obstacles to, radical change not only in the abstract general sense, but how one could practically get involved in bringing it about.

Problems of working 'inside' or 'outside' the system; of what was 'real' as opposed to cosmetic change; of what the characteristics of a just society were and the role of violence in changing or maintaining the status quo; these problems cropped up endlessly in seminars, symposia and discussion groups. My intellectual interest had shifted again to resolving the tension between analysis, commitment and practice; ie not only to analyse or to declare my commitment to certain values, but to find some practical way of pursuing the latter so that they made sense in terms of the former. All I know now, with more certainty and resignation than I knew then, is that it is not easy, and this problem still preoccupies me. At Cape Town and at Wits I began to develop the intellectual and moral uneasiness towards the 'grand' theories of social change that I felt towards the closed theological systems of the Divinity School. The dogmatic confidence, the academic pigheadedness of some of the Marxist and functionalist scholars, and particularly those students who were desperately searching for a secular eschatology, were no different from some of the devout souls at Stellenbosch who resolutely tried to take me on a mental route march through the Kingdom of God. Emotionally I felt 'a plague on the arrogance of both your creeds!'; intellectually I resorted to critical reasoning, searching for a way to come to terms with the problems posed.

Though the answers to many still elude me, I hope I have sharpened my ability to recognize some of those that are unacceptable.

The beginning of an answer to the question: 'How come you, an Afrikaner ...?' must be found in the experiences I have so inadequately referred to – and of course many others which elude both my memory or my ability to portray them. For example friends. Right throughout my stages of growth and development, Marcia, my twin sister, was an *alter ego* and emotional sounding board. Our bond remains indestructible. Then Dian Joubert, my first mentor at University, who even today tests my intellect and friendship with a freshness which never fails to challenge convention; the honour and courage of André du Toit and Hermann Giliomee; Anna-Hilge who strips the word 'individuality' of all cultish pretentiousness in the way she lives her daily life; Michael Savage who uses satire and wit to lighten the load of moral ambiguity and who gives friendship without reservation; Lawrence Schlemmer who refuses to give in to the complexity of life – he can keep more intellectually and morally contradictory balls in the air than any other person I know, and they are all genuine; the resolution of David Welsh to be a South African in his own right; Hennie Serfontein, my idea of a real Afrikaner; Theo Hanf, an extraordinary combination of towering intellect and compassion; Heribert Adam, a gentle man with a devotion to the systematic analysis of the South African problem, the passion of Ian Mac-

28

Donald for justice, E K Moorcroft, the gentle giant and old fashioned patriarchal family man, who has an infectious love of the soil and trees; and Ian Jones – what a great companion. It is wrong even to begin to do this, except perhaps to show how impossible it is to do it adequately and also how incomplete the answer would be without at least the attempt.

Even more difficult to account for and as important, is my primordial relationship with the Afrikaans language. I know that it has been called the language of the oppressor, the medium of apartheid, and there is some truth in that, but only a small part of the truth. It was also born out of a reaction to bondage and a desire for freedom and to release it from its present indignity is a worthy cause for those who wish to take it on. This is not my major concern, and does not explain my involvement with it. Language shapes one's social and personal identity and in that sense Afrikaans is my language. I can no more escape it (nor do I wish to) than deny my own existence.

The very fact that people can ask: 'How come you, an Afrikaner …?' is proof of it. I love to speak it, listen to it and share anecdotes, jokes and experiences in it. It is beautiful. I have been privileged to be a student of N P van Wyk Louw and D J Opperman and to have read their poetry. I am warmed by the exuberance of Jan Rabie whenever I meet him and the way in which he speaks it, and awed by the ability André Brink has to express ideas and concepts in it. I have also been deeply shamed and angered by the official hypocrisy and shallowness that has been conveyed by it. But, I can honestly say I have never been ashamed to speak it or to claim it as my first language. On the contrary, more often than not, I take pride in its being an authentically African language. It belongs nowhere else but on this continent. And yet, with Breyten Breytenbach and others I grieve and am apprehensive for its future. I shared a platform with him, Andrè Brink and others at the University of Cape Town Summer School of 1973 on *Die Sestigers* – a period of Afrikaans literature. Breyten had returned after thirteen years of self-imposed exile to give the keynote address. The hall was packed and the atmosphere charged, when, in a quiet voice, he told the story of the guide in the Cedarberg whose wife had died during the night on the mountain, a man torn between going for help and protecting her corpse from the leopards.

He used this story to explain why he, Breyten, still carried on writing in Afrikaans – to protect the corpse. I remember Schalk Pienaar, an esteemed Afrikaans and Nationalist Party-supporting journalist, sitting at the Press table weeping. I still cannot agree with Breyten that it is already a corpse, but continue to hope that its present disease does not prove to be terminal.

Well, that is the answer to the question and, of course, it is not the whole story. How can it ever be?

Becoming house-trained

The moment I was elected, my employment at the University ceased. Not so my obligations to some of my students and I agreed to carry on teaching until mid-year.

While I was preparing for the family's move to Cape Town after the election, Colin Eglin invited me to go with him on a trip to Nigeria and to stop over in Lusaka and Nairobi on the way. I accepted with alacrity, only afterwards realizing that the whole burden of moving to Cape Town and into a new house would come down on Mana's shoulders. Already I was sliding into a lifestyle where I began to attribute an urgency and necessity to requests on my time which eventually played havoc with my private life. In retrospect, I am not sure whether doing so was symptomatic of or responsible for the state of affairs of my marriage. Be that as it may, I accepted Eglin's invitation with excitement and enthusiasm.

The night before I departed to join him in Lusaka I had a public meeting in the Feathermarket Hall in Port Elizabeth. The next afternoon at three o'clock we were sitting in State House, Lusaka, having tea with President Kaunda. Initially the pace was bewildering: official cars, red carpets, outriders, chartered aircraft, everyone smiling, patting shoulders and looking like men of the world.

Kaunda is a disarming man; a gentle demeanour comes across with believable sincerity. He spoke with great emotion (at one stage weeping) about the virtues of 'political humanism', but I am afraid, apart from stressing that we should rid ourselves of prejudice and recognize each other's humanity, I simply could not get at what he was trying to say. Even then, one thing was quite clear, he posed no conceivable threat to South Africa. (A few months later, at my first session of Parliament, Eglin and I were attacked by the Minister of Defence, P W Botha, for consorting with 'rapists and murderers of our wives and children north of our borders'.)

We stayed with Zach and Mona de Beer. He was then in charge of

Anglo American's copper interests in Zambia and the evening after the interview with Kaunda was taken up by a dinner which Zach gave in our honour. A number of Kaunda's Cabinet Ministers and some diplomats were invited.

Two things stand out about that evening. The first was something I was to experience many times afterwards. To be a white South African was to be almost automatically typecast as an apologist for the status quo in South Africa. Inevitably, some social time had to be sacrificed to correct this error, but not before others had offloaded their anger or pet theory on why whites felt they needed apartheid and I had tried to explain my own attitude towards the domestic situation.

Establishing mutually acceptable bona fides seems to be a necessary ritual in political conversation for white South Africans, whether they tour Africa, abroad, or their own country.

The second thing I came across a few times on the rest of the trip: black/white marriages, usually black husbands and white wives. No matter how racially liberated I was, it was still strange for me to meet such couples. I tried to be appropriately mature and indifferent to the situation, but I somehow sensed they were aware that I was thinking about 'what it must be like'. Later on in the evening, one such husband, ex-Oxford golf captain and an up-and-comer in the Kaunda administration, swaying slightly with a liquid stalactite yo-yoing from his bottom lip, made a coarse reference to his wife who fortunately was out of earshot. His remark was one of those stereotype sexual innuendos that husbands sometimes indulge in to draw attention to their own virility or lack of it, but it served to give me some perspective. This marriage, like all others, was also a relationship with the same prospects of success or failure, acceptance or misunderstanding between the partners. There were of course special political and social circumstances which were relevant to such marriages. Many were concluded in the immediately post-colonial era and white wives were obvious status symbols.

At the time of our trip some of them, I sensed, were very lonely people and feeling slightly ostracized with the 'black is beautiful' fad being in vogue. But at the end of the trip I knew that the ratio of 'unhappy' to 'happy' marriages amongst such couples was about the same as in so-called 'unmixed' marriages. Charles Njonjo's marriage, from the brief evidence I had of it, appeared to be an extremely happy one.

He was then Attorney-General of Kenya and we stayed in his home the next night in Nairobi. He and his family left for his country retreat on our arrival and Eglin and I had the run of his house. We gathered that it was not prudent for him to be seen entertaining two white politicians from South Africa as there were some local elections on at the time. Njonjo is a black Englishman from his Oxford accent to his pinstripe suit. One of the rare beneficiaries of accumulated tribal wealth (he was the son of a wealthy chief), he lived in an enormous mansion with the missionary's daughter he had married and their children. All the signs of a comfortable and happy family life were in evidence. The residence would have nestled quite naturally in any of the élite Northern suburbs of Johannesburg, with the difference that in Nairobi the disturbing signs of abject poverty were only a few hundred metres from the front gate and not confined to an out-of-sight township. Much later that evening Eglin and I were sipping Njonjo's Napoleon brandy in his cosy bar with two enormous ivory tusks at the entrance, philosophizing about the circulation of élites and the redistribution of wealth in post-colonial Africa. (At the time of writing Njonjo is being charged with treason and conspiring against the State. A more unlikely conspirator is hard to imagine).

The next afternoon found us on the PAN-AM flight to Lagos. Two hundred tourists boarded as well. Safari hats with leopardskin bands made it clear they had been given the 'treatment' in their introduction to African wild life. As if by command they collectively removed their shoes and a sweet-sour stench wafted through the aircraft. Whichever way I turned my head my cheeks puckered at the assault from the smell. It was a desperate flight and I was ready to touch down in the pit of hell by the time we landed at Lagos at about seven that evening.

Eglin and I were a bit apprehensive as to the kind of reception we could expect in Nigeria. We were certainly not prepared for the popping of flashbulbs that blinded us down the boarding platform or the subsequent press conference. In the VIP lounge about two dozen journalists with microphones, TV cameras and tape recorders subjected us to some aggressive but not unfriendly questioning. It was a repeat of the Lusaka evening to a large extent.

'Apartheid is a white South African invention. You are a white

South African. So how do you justify your invention?' The underlying concern for democratic values implied in the questions was important and amusing. The absence in South Africa of universal franchise, majority rule and habeas corpus was vehemently deplored by them, at a time when Nigeria was being governed by a military junta where the same values were not much in evidence.

Afterwards we were swept into a lurching, bucking and weaving procession towards central Lagos. In the street every conceivable mode of transport, from mammy-wagons to donkeys, competed. An hour-and-a-half of this and we booked into the Federal Palace Hotel. The chauffeur and hotel reservations made it clear that everything was on the house and that we were guests of honour. It was Saturday night and a band was playing with couples ballroom dancing. Whenever a couple performed sufficiently well in the opinion of the audience or a section of it, someone would come forward and stick a note of currency onto the sweaty head of the male partner, to the enthusiastic applause of those who agreed. The humidity was oppressive, but there was a mood of exuberance throughout the evening.

I remember thinking that a few months ago I was an academic writing a paper in the superintendent's house at Modderfontein Sanatorium – and now here I was at the Federal Palace in Lagos, the MP for Rondebosch. There was no self-evident career path between the two and certainly no motivational consistency on my part which made any sense of it. In many ways I was in transition and I felt a heightened awareness brought about by the unfamiliarity of new experiences.

The next week was a compressed stacking up of appointments, sensations and incidents. Nothing challenges comfortable attitudes quite like a diversity of situations following one another without interruption in a short space of time.

From Sunday to Sunday –

Playing golf with Brigadier Ally, Chief of Lagos High Command. I am useless. Hacking away in the rough, my caddy asks me to talk to Dr Obu, my partner, and ask him to sponsor him (my caddy) for a career in the Civil Service. He explains that if this happens he has to pay ten per cent of his salary to his sponsor for the rest of his life. Not a bad system because the sponsor has a vested interest in his promotion (since it increases the quantity of the ten per cent). The caddy patiently explains that it is impossible to get a job in the Civil Service otherwise and that at present he is a tailor during the week, a caddy over weekends, studying for his Standard VIII exams and feeding a wife and four children. He is twenty-eight. Dr Obu laughed and shrugged his shoulders when I tried to steer the conversation in that direction.

Lagos has a huge squatter city. After the Ibo-Hausa war there was an influx of a million-and-a-half people. A squatter community is an example of human ingenuity under conditions of extreme stress and deprivation. It is difficult to imagine the problem of survival in an urban environment being more severely exposed. In Lagos this challenge has been met, if not necessarily won, with infectious exhiliration. I wandered for hours through the alleys, stalls and shacks. At night the fire *konkas* burned for the frying of small kebabs and yam cakes, loudspeakers howled and thumped, carts were wheeled by people shouting out the quality of the contents. One book cart had Kant's *Critique of Pure Reason* lying next to the *ABC of English Grammer*, and the boy selling them knew nothing of either. But what the hell. He was surviving, not teaching. I came across a man in a white toga carrying a long low bench and a blackboard and started talking to him. He was a freelance teacher – he offered parents to teach their children to read and write for a fee and guaranteed to do so within a specified time. If not he was fired. I imagined how this free market discipline would weed out the academic debris choking our universities in South Africa.

Despite the obvious problems of hygiene, the population density and residential crowding, I was convinced that the key elements to coping with third world urban housing problems were to be found in the manner in which the squatters of Lagos survived. In South Africa we destroyed squatter communities, forbade informal trade and teaching because it offended the official ideological sense of it. A mud hut in the rural area could be the legitimate and charming subject for a photograph of traditional Africa, but was seen as an offensive contradiction of antiseptic suburbia in the urban areas. Influx control was our pathetic and useless attempt to persuade ourselves that we were coping better than the rest of the Third World with the problems of urbanization. What a hangover we were preparing for ourselves.

On the third day our Ibo chauffeur told us that he would no longer be driving for us. He had been undercut by a Yoruba, who promised the Hausa foreman of the driving pool that he could get fifty per cent of our tip when we left. The Hausa and Ibo had just come through a bad civil war. We gave the Ibo chauffeur a generous tip which we subtracted from the tip we gave the slimy Yoruba and hoped it would get him into the stew with the Hausa foreman. Nobody can tell us whiteys from the South anything about keeping ethnic vibrations alive.

Midweek saw us flying with Nigerian Airways to Enugu, capital of the Ibo and headquarters of Ojukwu, leader of the Ibos during the civil war. It was obviously an attempt to show us how reconstruction had progressed after the destruction caused by the conflict. We were met by a very nattily dressed gentleman called Ukaegbu. He had a white suit, brown shoes and spats on and I was constantly awed by how he managed to walk through the red mud and dust of Enugu without getting a spot on his suit or spats – particularly the way he lifted his feet when walking through the very dusty parts. I dubbed him *Flashgat* Ukaegbu. He was a remarkably hospitable guide and chaperone. That evening we were the guests of honour of the Administrator of the region, a Dr Okwu-i-Okwu, PhD Oxford.

It was a posh and extravagant feast given the surroundings and circumstances in which we enjoyed it. Towards the end of the evening *Flashgat* drew me aside, winked and whispered that he was taking Eglin and myself to a night club for some fun and games. I could not imagine a night club in Enugu, but half an hour later we were in a cellar dive with strobe lights flashing, shriek-thumping music and grinding, bumping and stomping figures on the dance floor and between tables. We drank Coke laced with cane from small bottles. There were about four women to every man, most of them very young teenage girls. They unashamedly came up and took you for a dance. Talking was impossible. *Flashgat* told me in the toilet that most of them were orphans from the civil war trying to survive through prostitution. The strobe lights blinded me and I tried to get the rhythm with two Ibo orphans and I laughed. Back at the table *Flashgat* whispered that Eglin and I could have as many of the girls for the night as we fancied. I could see an international incident in the making: 'White South African MP refuses Ibo prostitute', so I passed the buck by saying that Eglin was my leader and that it would be presumptuous of me to decide ahead of him on such a weighty issue. *Flashgat* moved across to Eglin and I watched him closely. His eyes widened momentarily when the import of the message hit home, but being a top-drawer politician he pleaded fatigue on behalf of both of us and we were off the hook. God save us from a civil war. There were some brutalized human beings in that cellar dive of Enugu.

Back in Lagos we sought an interview with President Gowon. It was an on-off situation for forty-eight hours, but finally we were told to wait with our luggage at a certain garage at eight-thirty on Saturday morning. We had an eleven o'clock flight to Madrid to connect with an SAA flight to Johannesburg. At eight forty-five a black Mercedes arrived and took us to a barracks where Gowon lived. It was literally red carpet from the moment we got out of the car until we were in Gowon's office. He had a pleasant, open face, clipped moustache and military bearing. And he talked, from the moment we sat down until we left, about South Africa and Nigeria, the two giants of Africa at polar opposites ideologically and geographically; the need to pool their talents; the evils of racism, exploitation, colonialism. My watch said ten fifteen and I gave up on our flight. We were stuck in Lagos for a few more nights. There was no way we were going to make it to the airport. It had taken us an hour-and-a-half to get to the Federal Palace Hotel when we arrived.

At ten twenty Gowon looked at his watch and said we had better leave for our flight. Eglin and I smiled politely and said we thought we had missed it. Gowon disagreed and he was right. He gave us two outriders and with screaming sirens we howled back to the airport. It was amazing what effect these Presidential outriders had. Everyone scattered and those who did not were literally kicked out of the way. At ten fifty we were in our seats for the flight to Madrid. Three months later Gowon was toppled by a coup and became a Political Science student in England.

From Lagos to Madrid. That evening we sat in a fancy Spanish restaurant eating European food and watching cabaret. The experiences and the contradictions of the last week, up to that very moment, were still too immediate and alive for me to synthesize them. But one thing I do remember feeling very strongly, and this has stayed with me ever since – I was of and from Africa. Not in some silly romantic *Snows of Kilimanjaro* sense, but first in the realization that I was not a European. The Spanish restaurant reinforced this awareness very strongly. But also in the sense in which the problems of the continent, of South Africa, occupied my mind, my thoughts, my time. I have always been fascinated by the contingency of birth and the inevitability of death, and particularly by the arbitrariness of my particular spot on the earth where through force of circumstance, habit and perhaps inclination, I spend my life. Africa had me whether I was content or not. The next day we were back in Johannesburg.

The first major issue which involved me as a parliamentarian was the squatter problem. The '75 Session saw the introduction of the Prevention of Illegal Squatting Amendment Bill: a straightforward, brutal, punitive measure, devoid of any planning or awareness of the problems of urbanization. Two squatter communities had already been demolished in the Cape Flats area, and a new one, Crossroads, was under threat. Alex Boraine and I drove out to Crossroads to see the situation firsthand and to meet some of the inhabitants. The contrasts to Lagos were too stark not to be noticed. Crossroads stood isolated away from the city, cut off from its benefits.

In addition to the normal hardships of this kind of existence there was constant harassment by officialdom who demanded that the people go back where they came from. They never tried to understand why the squatters were there in the first place. The vast majority were women and children who through economic circumstance left rural areas to join their migrant labourer husbands.

During a visit to KTC, a squatter camp adjacent to Crossroads, one of the husbands implored me to go to his shack. On the wall was a certificate of merit for fifteen years' loyal service to his company. He had left the single quarters in Langa, a black township, to provide shelter for his wife and children who had suddenly arrived from rural Transkei. They already had three children. His wife became pregnant and bore triplets. The birth partially paralysed her and the husband went to the rural Transkei to marry a nurse, according to traditional custom, to come and look after the wife and six children. All he wanted from me was to go to the relevant Minister and assure him that he, the husband, was a hardworking man and meant no harm and that this was the most practical and economical way of coping with his predicament.

He was of course absolutely right, but the authorities insisted that he put his wife in a nursing home (where, for God's sake?), that he return to the single quarters and that the nurse-mother and six children go back to the Transkei. While he was commanding his wife to drag herself across the floor of the shack to prove to me that she was incapacitated an official entered the shack and told me that I was under arrest for being there without a permit. I told him I could not care less and that they could deliver a summons on me if they wished. This they duly did, I appeared in court, was found guilty, cautioned and discharged. I tried unsuccessfully to get an appointment with the relevant Minister and never saw the squatter husband and his family again. The appalling ignorance and indifference displayed in the debates in Parliament on the whole issue of squatting incensed me. But I soon learned that my sense of individual outrage was of absolutely no consequence in politics. I had to control my anger and probe for the weak spots and perhaps, if lucky, I could make some contribution in solving a problem. Ten years later Crossroads is still there and internationally famous. It has been joined by many other 'Crossroads' scattered all over the country. The Government has been overwhelmed by the inevitability of urbanization and has accepted the idea of emergency housing. The socio-economic hangover has begun.

I was awarded a cultural exchange travel scholarship by the American Government and in November 1975 I was in Washington attending a meeting addressed by our Ambassador to the United Nations, Mr Pik Botha, and an expatriate Methodist Minister called Danny Morton. The latter accused South Africa of invading Angola and trying to influence the composition of the first post-colonial Government in that country. I remember feeling somewhat sorry for Danny Morton because in his exile he had become the victim of anti-South African propaganda and was misinformed on the motives of the South African Government. I could not fault Pik Botha when he vehemently denied all the allegations and had to agree with him that the South African Government would be out of their minds to even contemplate such a venture. Early in January 1976, a delegation of parliamentarians was flown up to the operational area in Namibia to get a firsthand briefing. I was one of them. We flew in Louis Luyt's private jet. He is the fertilizer king in South Africa and the jet was plush with vulgar opulence – velvet easy chairs, gold-plated taps and so on. We visited Calueque, Ruacana, Rundu, Grootfontein and ended up in Oshikati.

Across the river from Rundu was the Angolan village of Calais. We were taken there to meet the refugees fleeing from the civil war raging in Angola.

It was essentially a power struggle between the MPLA, UNITA and FNLA to fill the vacuum created by the indecently hasty departure of the Portuguese. The refugees were mostly Portuguese colonials and mulattos. They had lost everything and desperately wanted entry into South Africa. I was very impressed with the way the South African Defence Force was assisting them in their plight even though we were not involved or obliged to do so. This naïveté on my part was soon demolished. At Oshikati, in the study of the Commissioner General of Ovamboland, the Chief of the Defence Force, General Magnus Malan, and General Constand Viljoen, in calm and measured tones, explained to us how the South African Defence Force had invaded Angola in August 1975 and were presently approximately 125 km from Luanda.

Danny Morton had been right after all. Fear was a warm glow in my abdomen as I realized that Shamus (my half-brother) must be involved in Angola somewhere. He was in charge of a Panhard armoured car and I understood why we had not heard from him in four months. Sitting opposite me in a Landrover after the briefing was Magnus Malan.*

'Well', he said, 'what do you think?'

I said I thought it was the greatest stupidity I could think of, that it was totally indefensible that we should be involved in determining the government of another country and that it violated the international principle of non-interference which South Africa had tirelessly insisted on for so long. All Malan said was that the Defence Force could evacuate completely within forty-eight hours if necessary. I asked

* Chief of Defence Force, later Minister of Defence.

him where the Panhard Armoured Division was likely to be and he replied that it was most likely deep into Angola.

The Landrover was on its way to a reception for us. There we were met by the Minister of Defence, P W Botha. The evening was bizarre. P W Botha was flushed with excitement. At one stage he said that if it were not for the presence of the Cubans he could take Luanda tomorrow. He went on to say, 'in fact, not only Luanda, but Lagos, Cairo and the whole of Africa'. Before the briefing I would have thought it all a joke. The next morning, flying back to Cape Town, we were told that the information given to us the previous day was classified and that we could not use it for any public or political purpose. I was numb with disbelief and with the fact that I had been involuntarily compromised into a deception of such magnitude. But more was still to come.

In *Time* and *Newsweek* one could read everything that the Generals had briefed us on in Oshikati, but our own newspapers were heavily censored on their reports of the Angolan conflict.

While the official Government view was that we were NOT involved in Angola I went across to the H F Verwoerd Building and asked General Constand Viljoen how a Panhard armoured car would fare against a Russian T54 tank. He said that as long as it did not rain it would be all right because the Panhard was more manoeuvrable. The next day it was raining in Angola and I was thinking of Shamus. During the No Confidence Debate the Prime Minister, the Minister of Defence and the Minister of Foreign Affairs got up and flatly denied that we were involved in the Angolan civil war. This was straightforward deception on the most elementary level.

When I tried to circumvent the constriction of talking about classified information by couching our involvement in Angola in hypothetical terms during the Defence Vote, the same P W Botha who spoke to me in such a friendly fashion in Oshikati lost his temper and raged at me that I would never again be invited to the operational area and that I was devoid of all patriotism. This kind of gobbledy-gook logic and inverted morality made *Alice in Wonderland* uncomplicated reading.

My experience of the Angolan débâcle had a fundamental influence on me. It made my transition into politics complete and toughened me to its pitfalls. I knew firsthand that governments could get away with murder if the circumstances were right; that people could be misled or deliberately deceived on a massive scale and worse; that even if they understood what had happened, they would not necessarily censure those who were responsible. I also learnt how easy it is to find yourself an unwilling co-conspirator in perpetrating the indefensible. If you were in opposition in South Africa, I began to understand, you needed iron in the soul not to lose faith in what you believed or lose sight of your objectives. You had to keep plugging away patiently without the prospects of immediate reward and always be prepared for failure and disappointment. But I also knew then what I believe now. No deception, grand or small, can endure indefinitely. The cracks will show and when they do it is better to search for more light than to perpetuate the darkness.

Race classification

Much has been said about the concept of apartheid and like most concepts with an enduring career in political discourse it ends up meaning
more or less what the ideological preferences of its users indicate. But
in its crudest generic sense, it literally means separateness or apart-
ness or setting apart. As a political slogan it fired the imagination of
the supporters of Afrikaner Nationalism and helped them to political
victory in 1948. Since then the South African Government has been
politically involved in setting up or undoing the consequences of
measures inspired by the concept of apartheid.

One such measure which is crucial to the understanding of the
racial structuring of an apartheid society such as South Africa, is the
Population Registration Act of 1950. It is popularly known as the
'Race Classification Act' because one of its most obnoxious pro-
visions is that it classifies every born and living South African according to either a race or an ethnic group or both. Without it, the peculiar
racial ordering of our society would be impossible. Other apartheid
measures depend on it for their implementation, such as the Separate
Amenities Act which allocates public facilities on a racial basis (how
can you allocate without knowing for whom to allocate?) and the
Group Areas Act which distributes land for residential and other purposes on a racial basis. No wonder one enthusiastic Nationalist referred to the Race Classification Bill as the Magna Carta of race relations for South Africa when it was introduced.

Nothing inspires as much vituperation towards South Africa domestically and internationally as the existence and consequences of this
law. It unites socialist and capitalist countries against us; it brings
about a unity of purpose between rich and poor, East and West, in
their opposition to us. White South Africa could establish a socialist
Utopia; it could have the highest growth rate and per capita income
under a free enterprise system imaginable; it could have solved the
problems of colonialism and underdevelopment, but as long as its

Government continues to insist that this law remains on the statute-books, apartheid as a political concept will never die and South Africa will never be spared the consequences of its existence. And why should it expect to be? Today there are Nationalist politicians who appeal to others not to use the word apartheid because it associates South Africa with the negative and distorted connotations evoked by this term. But you do not have to be unnecessarily negative or given to distortion to assess objectively and soberly that this law is fundamentally evil, racist and grossly discriminatory in its concept, implementation and consequence. Even if no one ever used the word apartheid any more, the effects of this law would evoke the same feelings of moral revulsion.

Why? Because essentially it denies voluntary association of the most elementary kind between individuals. True, poverty and exploitation limit the freedom of association of the individual as well, but this law prevents even the poor and exploited from associating with one another if they do not belong to the same race or ethnic group. One could even argue that some deserve to be rich or poor, but only crackpots or cranks would justify the deliberate social, political and economic consequences of being classified black or white or Coloured at birth.

This law not only prohibits the most elementary forms of human association: eating, sleeping, walking, talking, playing (in fact where such exceptions are being made today it is seen to epitomize reform and South Africa to be 'taking steps in the right direction'), but compounds this felony against human interaction by structuring most of the expectations and pursuits of the individual along channels of racial privilege. Thus, once you have been classified, it is predetermined which neighbourhood you will live in, what community facilities are at your disposal and which schools, public transport and occupational opportunities will be accessible to you. To complete the picture, this structure of racial privilege is serviced every year by a budget which is passed in a Parliament where the white political party, which has the largest number of supporters, dominates the key sites of decision making. And Cabinet Ministers are even today sometimes offended, when 'kindly disposed' foreigners suppress a smile of disbelief after the same Cabinet Ministers unctuously state that it is time the other racial groups started pulling themselves up by their own bootstraps 'like the Afrikaner did' and stopped expecting 'handouts' from the whites.

Perhaps this is the most pernicious consequence of the law: those that benefit most from it economically and socially are on the average oblivious of the advantages they enjoy because of its existence. Obviously this law is not the *cause* of poverty, exploitation, racism or racial inequality. These problems exist in many other societies. But this law makes it clear that these problems *have* to be institutionalized as a necessary part of the social order. It gives racial superiority legal sanction and feeds the illusion that you are better or worse because of the colour of your skin.

That is the difference, and that is the essence of apartheid, whatever the good intentions of those who conceived of it initially. Some argue sanctimoniously that, because of the fact that we have such laws, we are at least honest about our racism, whereas other societies are hypocritical. Our problem, it is said, is that we are too honest. This kind of perverted logic and morality stretches credulity – to strip law of justice and proclaim this a virtue. We must do away with the problems of racism and racial inequality, not sanctify them in law.

Ah, but our legislators were not without mercy when they conceived the Population Registration Act. Section 5(4) (c) actually lays down the conditions under which you can change your racial identity. The Magna Carta of race relations does allow for little enclaves of ambiguity and doubt. It is possible to change from white to Coloured or vice-versa. It is of course impossible to change from white to black or vice versa for obvious reasons, and generally speaking the natural inclination is to want to change up the ladder of racially constructed privilege, rather than down; to 'try for white', as it is known.

Section 5(4) (c) stipulates three conditions in terms of which one's application for a change of racial identity has to be considered – (a) ancestry, (b) appearance and (c) acceptance by the community. All the evidence is duly considered by a Race Classification Board and it pronounces on the success or failure of an application. But this is the culmination of a process riddled with humiliating pitstops before the race is won. An official from the Department of Internal Relations is assigned to the applicant's case. First comes the straightforward physical inspection. Does the applicant (and next of kin) 'look' Coloured or white? Photographs go to the Race Classification

Board, as well as copies of all other relevant identity documents: birth certificates of the applicant, or his parents, children, wedding certificates, driver's licences and so on.

Who were the parents, brothers and sisters? All this is carefully written down in a report. Finally the applicant's acceptance by the racial community of which he/she hopes to become a member has to be determined, or perhaps even the rejection or indifference of the racial community from which the applicant wishes to be 'declassified'. Statements from the neighbours (do you think of X as Coloured or white?); written references from Ministers of religion, employer, chairman of the sports club, even a visit to the applicant's regular pub for statements – all these are gathered for a report to the Race Classification Board. Finally, all the evidence as required by Section 5(4) (c) of the Population Registration Act is considered and a judgement given. How does this work in practice? Consider the following:

Soloman B is a Mozambican black. In 1951 he started to work as a waiter in the Clifton Hotel where he met and fell in love with a Coloured woman. In 1976 he came to see me with his 'boss' to find out whether he could be classified Coloured so that his children could have 'a better chance in life'. The 'boss' told me that Soloman B had come to him after he had left the Clifton Hotel and had worked loyally and efficiently for him ever since – 'one of the best drivers I have ever had'. With obvious pride Soloman B told me that he and his wife had brought up their three children properly, that they were all reborn Christians and he an elder in the Church.

He assured me that he himself could not care less about his racial identity, but 'for the sake of the children' he would like to be classified Coloured so that their racial identity could be cleared up and their life chances improved.

Soloman B's story did not quite make sense. According to Section 5(4) (c) Soloman B did not stand the whisper of a chance. His ancestry is black from Mozambique; his appearance is a black as the void in the Bermuda Triangle and his acceptance by the community as Coloured could be credibly expected only from the Christian fellowship of his church group. In fact, in terms of Section 5(4) (c) his children stood a better chance than their father of being classified Coloured, and certainly did not need the father's reclassification as the only basis for success. At least one of the parents, the mother, was Coloured; possibly they look more Coloured than their father and there would be a greater likelihood of wider community acceptance than in the Church only. In any case, Soloman B kept referring to 'his wife' and I thought at the time it was not possible for them to be legally married in terms of the Prohibition of Mixed Marriages Act. However, if he did have a marriage certificate this could improve the chances of his application. I asked him when he had married and if he had a copy of his marriage certificate.

He sat there as if I had kicked him in the face. Then slowly he stood up, looking at the ground and began weeping silently. Eventually huge gusty sobs doubled him up and down like someone who had the bends. In between he managed to tell me that this was the source of his undying shame. He had never (because he could not) legally married his wife. His children and the congregation did not know, but 'God knew' and he simply could no longer live with his conscience. In the same way he could not expect his wife to become a black so that they could marry as this would 'spoil the children's chances', and they might lose them. The only way for them to get legally married was for him to become a Coloured. That was why he had come to see me and he promised to pray for me every day if I would try and help him.

The 'boss' and I avoided each other's eyes in the embarrassment of the situation. Lamely I tried to explain to Soloman B that God had not made the Race Classification Act; that living twenty-five years with the mother of his children the way he had should surely convince God that Soloman B was an honourable man who held marriage in very high esteem. In fact, the respect of the congregation and of his children was more than sufficient evidence of this. And so on and so on. But Soloman B was adamant. In the eyes of God he was not legally married and as a devout Christian and elder of the Church he was deceiving the congregation as well as his children.

I said I would see what I could do, but I knew his case was hopeless. Nevertheless I wrote an impassioned letter to Dr Connie Mulder who was then the Minister of Internal Affairs, stating the case of Soloman B in full.

Three or so months later, in a day of extraordinary coincidence, the afternoon post arrived while I was talking to a student from UCT. He was from one of the most prominent Afrikaans families in Cape Town and wanted desperately to be reclassified Coloured because he had fallen deeply in love with a Malay Coloured girl. He sat on the edge of his chair quivering with tension. I told him it was usually easier to be classified 'down' than 'up' but given his background I did not think it would be possible. I asked him whether he was prepared to marry under Muslim rights (sometimes this can be more difficult than to be reclassified) and told him to do so and live with his Muslim wife in a Coloured group area. As far as I know that is precisely what he did.

After he had left, I opened the post. In his wisdom, or lack of it, Dr C Mulder, the Minister of Internal Affairs, had decided that Soloman B could become a Coloured. It made no sense in terms of Section 5(4) (c), but I was delighted for Soloman B that he could marry the mother of his children after living with her for twenty-five years.

But one Sunday afternoon at about four o'clock the granddaddy (literally) of a race classification case stood on my doorstep. With him was a son-in-law. They had not been in my study for more than five minutes stating their case when it became clear that an inspection *in loco* was unavoidable. The father-in-law, let us call him Bodenstein (for it was an Afrikaans name of that length and sound), agreed to assemble his family two evenings hence. In the meantime he left some documents and his own covering memo for me to study.

In 1952 or thereabouts, he had been a waiter on the South African Railways when he met and married a Coloured woman. He knew that it was not legal to marry, but as he wrote (and repeated many times afterwards), a 'law cannot stop people from loving one another' and he and his wife were very much in love and never anticipated what consequences would follow for them or for their children. So Mr Bodenstein forged his wedding certificate to make it look like a legitimate one. He could not forge his wife's identity document though, but for some of the children he forged birth certificates, and others he did not register. Mr Bodenstein, being a healthy normal working class white, was not going to spend too much time underpinning the prevailing official ideology; he was more interested in getting on with the job of living.

However, things came to a head and Mr Bodenstein's ingenuity went through a lean patch. One of his sons-in-law, let us call him Weideman, a crane driver in the Cape Town docks who had married one of Mr Bodenstein's daughters with a dubious birth certificate, tried to register the birth of his second child. The first one's register

48

came up white but the second one came up Coloured. Mr Bodenstein, flushed with the success of one of his grandchildren surviving the whiteness test, applied for the Book of Life for all the ambiguous children. Some came up white, others Coloured.

'Please help me', he said. 'Some of the grandchildren are on the point of going to school and you know Coloured schools are not as good as white ones. In any case my one daughter wants to get married to a white and her Book of Life came up wrong for her.'

The following Tuesday evening I went to Mr Bodenstein's house in Woodstock/Observatory, a working-class white area. On the wall were chocolate-coloured pheasants flying off into a turquoise sunset over some pine trees, and there was a rearing black stallion in porcelain on the colour television. Twenty-seven members of the family were present: Mr Bodenstein and his wife, their children and grandchildren. I explained to them exactly what they could expect from the Department of Internal Affairs while mentally putting each one of them through the 5(4) (c) test. This case had a lot of possibilities.

When I explained the 'community acceptance' condition there was some good-natured laughter and I realized that in the Woodstock/Observatory area there were not too many pots who were going to call kettles Coloured. I asked each adult if he/she was prepared to go through the indignity of an investigation and they all declared themselves ready to do battle. By the time I left I had a diagram of a family tree that would make the line authority flow chart of a multinational company look simple.

I sent all the identity documents plus a genealogical diagram with a covering letter to the Minister. In my letter I suggested two options to him. He could declare the grandmother white and everything would be solved. The very fact that Mr Bodenstein and his wife were legally white made all their offspring white immediately. It would take his Department very little time. However, if he was not prepared to classify the grandmother white, I was determined to apply for each individual case in the file. This would involve a great deal of time and energy. A Deputy Minister of Internal Affairs had been appointed in the meantime and part of his duty was to deal with race classification cases. His name was Pen Kotze. The better I had got to know him the more I have liked him. We have always been extremely blunt, almost insulting to each other and we have never made any secret about what we think of each other's political stance.

To his credit, Pen Kotze has never tried to soften the stark nature of white political domination in his dealings with me. He has a cynical sense of tragedy about the untenability of his political position, but unless a watertight alternative is presented to him he is not going to let anyone else dominate better than he can. I remember teasing him the day Matanzima of the Transkei broke off diplomatic relations with South Africa.

I said, 'Well, Pen, what do you say about your own home-made foreign country poking a finger in your eye?'

He just laughed and replied, 'That little kaffir had better watch it or we'll take his porridge away.'

He had received my letter on the Bodenstein/Weideman case and when he saw me in the lobby he shook his head and said I was making it very difficult for him. He could not classify the grandmother white, that would be 'cooking the books' too much, but he said he was pre-pared to make a deal. He speaks with a pronounced Malmesbury bray, which means he rolls all his r's in the back of his throat. He smiled and said he could not make them all white now because then there would be too many 'Progs' (PFP supporters) in the Maitland constituency. He was prepared to make half white now and the rest over the next few years. It took five years in all for the Bodenstein/ Weideman tribe to become legally white. (By the way, between Jan-uary 1981 and June 1983:

1742 Cape Coloureds	were changed to white
22 whites	were changed to Cape Coloured
26 whites	were changed to Chinese
5 blacks	were changed to Indian
8 blacks	were changed to other Asian)

In my own dealings with such cases I have had more failures than successes.

I think of a white mother with a deceased Coloured husband des-perately tarting up her two daughters with powder and hair straight-ener and an attractive Coloured electrician living with his white wife and baby in my own constituency. The house is in her name and he pretends to be on a duty call when strangers appear.

They have sympathetic and understanding neighbours. Another

couple moved to Windhoek, Namibia, for a better future for their children, but had to return because the husband could not find a job. These are unpretentious, unpublic people. I could not help them. There are more well known dramatic examples as well. Gentle and intelligent Rick Turner who, with Fozia, had the courage to live together and demonstrate their commitment and love publicly until he was assassinated. And then, of course, Breyten and Yolande Breytenbach. Anyone who has read what he has written, or spoken to either, will know that the Population Registration Act and its consequences have marred their lives like burning tar.

I know that those who profess a concern for reform and support 'steps in the right direction', will chide me for writing in this fashion.

'Why focus on the negative and the exceptional?'

'Why not show what is positive and good, however small?'

'Are we not moving away from that kind of nonsense?'

'Look at what has happened to the Prohibition of Mixed Marriages Act and Section 16 of the Immorality Act.'

Such attitudes simply obscure the dilemma of undertaking genuine reform. I welcomed the scrapping of the Prohibition of Mixed Marriages Act and Section 16 of the Immorality Act.

But these acts are simply *some* of the consequences of the Population Registration Act. In any racially mixed society multi-ethnic marriages are the exception rather than the rule. With these Acts we have not only highlighted the exceptional nature of these marriages or love affairs, but made their very existence a crime. Anybody in his right mind would welcome some return to sanity by scrapping these Acts and sparing those involved in such relationships the humiliation and heartache which they have caused.

But it would be extremely superficial to think that we have more than scratched the surface of reform by scrapping these Acts. The Population Registration Act is the generic act structuring racial privilege over a wide range of activities of which sexual intercourse and marriage across the colour lines happen to be the sensational exceptions. It is in the competition for jobs, land, schools, houses, that the real sense of racial deprivation and discrimination is kept alive, and a source of explosive political, economic and social conflict as well. Nothing competes with the Population Registration Act in drawing the racial lines of this conflict.

Nowhere is this demonstrated more vividly than in the political application of this Act to the South African Coloured and Indian people. The Coloureds and Indians do not represent political groupings in any ethnic or cultural sense of the word. In fact, in the Indian community the cleavage between Hindu and Muslim is greater than anything that exists between Afrikaans- and English-speaking whites. Similarly, there is enough research evidence to demonstrate quite clearly that Coloureds have no distinctive sense of cultural homogeneity setting them off from that which exists amongst whites. However, the Population Registration Act forces Coloureds and Indians to participate politically as involuntary racial groups. It is not considered relevant that there are natural political groupings among them, believing in capitalism, socialism, Western civilization or even white domination. Whatever the political differences amongst them, the Population Registration Act forces them to participate politically as Coloureds or Indians. Why? Because it enables the dominant white minority to structure political competition in their own favour by making artificial minorities of the Coloureds and Indians. But in doing this the white minority institutionalizes the problem of group domination and makes it even more intractable to resolve. And the final irony now is that the new constitution entrenches the problem of racial domination which flows from the existence of the Population Registration Act. In fact, the new constitution cannot operate without this Act and apartheid is going to be with us as long as this is the case.

Political leadership

I became Leader of the Progressive Federal Party and of the official Opposition in Parliament in September 1979. I did so reluctantly and with apprehension. After five years in Parliament as a back bencher, I knew exactly what I did not want. I definitely did not want to spend the rest of my productive days in the South African Parliament. There cannot be many institutions that steal time so quietly and unobtrusively; that can drag you into a rhythm that has a sense of boring necessity; imposes a feeling of mindless obligation and keeps alive an indefinable but compelling *esprit de corps* towards your colleagues, both likeable and unlikeable. Half the year is gone in a flash. The rest is spent recovering and trying to catch up before you start again.

But it was not only Parliament. After five years I knew quite clearly that I was not cut out to be a public figure. I certainly did not enjoy the publicity and began to dread the many occasions where through force of circumstance and the need for emotional self-preservation I had to act in a pleasant, interested and ritual manner – congresses, cocktails and protocol dinners. I suppose any job has its unpleasant, obligatory side effects. But Parliament is not an occupation: it is an all-encompassing lifestyle posing as a career. Your life becomes part of the job, not the other way around.

To take on the leadership would intensify my involvement both as a parliamentarian and a public figure. Why did I do it? Part of the political tradition which I believe to be important for any country, but especially for my own, is protest. The legacy of Helen Suzman in Parliament is not analysis or the spelling out of alternatives or even being a 'good' parliamentarian or South African. She demonstrated that parliamentary protest in a situation of powerlessness and against all real political odds had its own dignity, relevance and moral compulsion. She prevented certain values, necessary for an open humane society, from being ignored: freedom of speech, association and movement, habeas corpus. She kept debate on them alive in a society that was trying to ignore them. Of course she was not the only one to do so, but she was one of the very few to do so in Parliament and I believe that this kind of protest needs to be kept alive in this form.

It is fashionable in radical left and fascist rightwing circles to dismiss these values as examples of liberal moral masturbation, the bleatings of tenderminded political consciences out of step with the forces of history. These are tired old arguments: Stalin and Hitler used them with equal vehemence and irrationality, and long after the world has either forgotten, or will still be avoiding the 'steps' they were so confident of, these values continue to form the motive force of political protest wherever individual freedom and human dignity are threatened or destroyed. The evidence that such is the case in South Africa is overwhelming. Protest has to be kept alive, and I cannot expect others to do it if I am not prepared to do it myself.

My concern for political protest is not the only consideration. If nothing else is left to do, then to protest is to do something, and it has to be done. But given the structural limitations of Parliament and its position in South African society, the question was whether or not other options than protest could be explored. When I came to Parliament, debate on political party policy alternatives had a well-worn and sterile quality. Whichever party, including the Progressive Party, propagated a constitutional policy *for* everyone else in the country. Because of the take-it-or-leave it nature of such proposals any rejection implied confrontation as the only alternative style of politics. Consequently, debates focused almost exclusively on constitutional *content* rather than constitutional *process*. Politicians argued about the viability of some 'final solution' to the existing dilemma instead of exploring ways of moving away from it.

Eglin, who was then Leader of the Progressive Federal Party, saw that we were going to be trapped into this sterile debate and was determined that we find ways to avoid this. He appointed me Chairman of the party's Constitutional Commission with the brief to formulate a new Constitutional policy for the party which would still incorporate the old principles, but would take new social, economic and political developments into account. This enabled me to give focus to the wide-ranging debates, analyses and seminars I had been involved in over the last few years. It was ironic, but intellectually the most challenging period for me (as far as analyzing African and South African

54

politics was concerned) developed after I had left academic life and become a full-time politician.

In this respect I was, and still am, extremely fortunate in having friendships with some analytically keen academics and students of the African and South African situation. For the purposes of devising some constitutional policy I was greatly influenced (though they may be totally blameless and unaware of it) by Theo Hanf and his co-workers from the Arnold Bergstraesser Institute in Freiburg; Arend Lijphart, now from the University of California, San Diego; Heribert Adam from Simon Fraser in Canada; Bill Johnston from Oxford; Du Toit, Degenaar and Gagiano from Stellenbosch; Ian MacDonald from Rhodes; and Lawrence Schlemmer from Natal University; as well as David Welsh, Mike Savage and Hermann Giliomee from UCT. Of course there were other academics as well, but I met the above frequently and at various venues where the same debates were carried on. Outside the academic community and with a lot of political wisdom gathered from the hustings, people like Zach de Beer, Japie Basson and Colin Eglin were a counterfoil to flights of academic fancy. Then there is Nic Olivier, an invaluable methodical mind, who, like me, had moved from academic life into white party politics and instinctively sensed my discomfort whenever dilemmas of moral and intellectual compromise presented themselves. I will always be grateful to him for allowing me to curse expediency in the privacy of his friendship.

As it happened I was offered a three-month Research Fellowship by the Institute for Social and Economic Research, at Rhodes University in Grahamstown shortly after Eglin appointed me as Chairman of the Constitutional Commission. This was a godsend and meant that I could work uninterruptedly in academic seclusion. I also managed – through the kind offices of Zach de Beer – to raise some money to hold a weekend seminar to which I could invite domestic and international academics to apply their minds to the problems that faced my party's Commission. It was an exhilarating time. Shortly afterwards my Commission concluded its work and reported to Eglin. He decided that he and I had to go on a campaign to prepare the party and the media for the acceptance of the report – as party policy – at a forthcoming National Congress.

I suppose this is the real cutting edge of the difference between academic and political life. A set of constitutional proposals can charm you intellectually by the manner in which they are consistent with their initial assumptions. I found our set of proposals intellectually charming. But the art of politics is to convert constitutional assumptions into political trends. I cannot speak for other societies, but in the South African context this is extraordinarily difficult. There are so many factors which contribute to gelling stereotypes and preconceived notions: racial and ethnic differences, economic inequality, regional and provincial differences: urban-rural, modern-traditional. This diversity was the socio-cultural infrastructure on which white politics played out its self-enclosed political one-acter. And even within white politics, there were factors which intensified misunderstanding and suspicion: in particular the language difference, which was still reflected in competing business and newspaper establishments. So for a start, I accepted as given that the Afrikaans newspaper and media establishment, with its links to the Nationalist Party, would be mercilessly devoted to shooting down proposals other than the official ones.

There would not be the time to persuade political organizations outside the confines of white politics to take our set of proposals seriously. To most of their spokesmen (particularly in black politics) we represented 'mink and manure' liberals who were either trying to 'have our cake and eat it' or had to demonstrate our integrity by capitulating our intellects and morals to indulge their sense of political deprivation or our own presumed sense of racial guilt.

This was driven home to me forcibly when, a few years later – after the proposals had been published and debated endlessly – some blacks present, in a private seminar in which I participated, insisted that the proposals were racist, despite the fact that they accepted I was not, and yet knew I had formulated the proposals. It was also clear to me that until then, they and most others present had not studied them in any serious way. This of course did not detract in any way from the vehemence and confidence with which we all participated in the discussion.

The game plan to convert our set of proposals from a charming tautology to part of a viable political debate was a limited one, given the scope of its recommendations. We had to persuade the English newspaper establishment to be sympathetic, if not converted, and then get the approval of our own party formations at a National Congress.

Then it was up to us in Parliament to force the debate there and in other opinion-forming forums in white politics. To the extent that the Government engaged us, some new ideas could by pumped into the tired, old and sterile debate of white politics.

Whatever the details of the set of constitutional proposals, and there are many which could be singled out for distortion and misrepresentation, Eglin and I felt very strongly that we should highlight *process* assumptions rather than *content* assumptions; assumptions that concentrated more on *how* to arrive at an acceptable constitution, than those that dealt with the details of such a constitution. From the outset we focused our arguments on the merits of a National Convention where a new acceptable constitution had to be formulated. Negotiation rather than consultation and prescription; consensus, rather than majority decision-making; no racial or group domination and no racial discrimination; individual participation through the franchise, were propagated from platform to platform. We pushed for negotiable and non-negotiable principles to introduce some flexibility into the constitutional debate. This was new and provocative in white politics in 1979.

In our discussions Eglin and I realized there would be two persistent obstacles which we would have to consider. Open-style negotiation politics would not be popular with dogmatists from either the right or the left. From the one we would be presented as 'sell-outs' of white interests; from the other we would be accused of sacrificing principle. The constitutional dogmatists from the right demanded copper-bottomed guarantees that whites would dominate in perpetuity; those from the left saw any divergence from one man one vote linked to majority rule as losing face with the blacks and 'betraying our liberal ideals'. The second obstacle, paradoxically, was that to the extent that the ruling establishment took over some of our ideas, our own relevance would be questioned by some of our traditional support groups. This remains an inevitable dilemma.

The constitutional proposals were accepted overwhelmingly at the party congress. In the meantime the Government had appointed a parliamentary Commission of Inquiry to investigate 'the formulation and introduction of a new constitution for the Republic of South Africa'. Eglin, Basson, Dalling and myself served on that Commission for the Progressive Federal Party and we sent our proposals to it as evidence. So, apart from my belief in the importance of political protest, I felt that we were poised on the brink of a new king of political debate in South Africa.

But there was another factor which was increasing in its significance for me. I remembered how as an academic concerned with problems of political change I had considered both violent and non-violent revolutionary/evolutionary theories of change with frivolous indifference. They were academic exercises for me. I introduced some assumptions, explored research findings, drew some tentative conclusions, stimulated or bored some students and went off to play squash or have a beer.

But the longer I had been in politics, the more I had met people who had either been the victims or the perpetrators of oppression and political violence: people from Algeria, Ireland, Lebanon, Cyprus, Eastern Europe, Latin America, Zimbabwe, Mozambique, Angola and of course South Africa. In discussions with them a few ideas began to crystallize very clearly: never talk lightly about violence as an instrument to change or maintain the status quo and never think you alone understand how political power works. In particular, I discovered that there were compelling similarities between the ideologies of revolution and domination. The élites in either case, once I had accepted their initial assumptions, could justify why individual human rights, accountable democratic politics, the rule of law, opposition, or freedom of the press had to be suspended or done away with altogether for the sake of the people, stability and order, the workers, or Western civilization.

Finally, there is no difference in the logic of the vanguard of the revolution which argues that some will have to die (very seldom any of their own) for the sake of the revolution and that of the dominating élite which states that unfortunately some will have to lose their freedom and will have to suffer (again, very seldom any from their own ranks) for the sake of order and stability for the majority. It is remarkable how a successful liberation élite becomes a reactionary dominant élite without so much as a gear shift in its ideological assumptions.

Nothing demonstrated it to me more vividly in recent times than the way a law which Ian Smith of Rhodesia had passed to absolve anti-terrorist actions by his soldiers was used by the Mugabe Government to absolve one of his men, Tekere, who had shot down a farmer in cold blood whilst busy with anti-terrorist actions. The shock registered by whites and the West was cyclopic hypocrisy. Both ideologies of revolution and domination, in their key assumptions, are anti-democratic, anti-individual and fundamentally irrational. So, when it comes to political power and its uses I am a philosophical conservative. (This conservatism must in no way be linked to any existing political party, and, of course, especially not to the Conservative Party of South Africa.)

I am conservative in believing that the use of political power must have as many democratic constitutional checks as possible. When it comes to political change, constitutional possibilities to bring it about must be explored until circumstance makes this impossible. Believing this, I had to support whichever such possibilities seemed plausible.

These were some of the underlying reasons which predisposed me towards accepting the position of Leader of the Progressive Federal Party and of the official Opposition. In fact, at the time I was becoming increasingly bored with Parliament and felt the need for a change. I certainly did not believe that the future of political protest, stimulating a new political debate, or keeping the vestiges of constitutional change alive, depended on my presence in Parliament. So when Dr Louis Babrow, a member of the Council of the University of Cape Town, invited me for lunch and asked me whether I was prepared to be nominated for the position of Principal of the University which would become vacant on Sir Richard Luyt's retirement, I said yes. Of course I was flattered at being asked but I never thought I stood more than an outside chance. I suppose saying yes reflected my state of mind about what I was doing at the time more than any alternative I was contemplating.

Eglin, as Leader of the Progressive Party, had managed through a series of negotiations to consolidate our position as the official Opposition. Since 1974, the United Party – which was then the official Opposition and was at one stage the Government of South Africa – had experienced a steady decline in electoral fortunes. It is difficult to imagine a political party anywhere that could be reduced to a state of political inertia by conflicting internal interest groups as quickly as the United Party. It misread every political cue in the book and appeared to believe that provided it did nothing in an unobtrusive way, some political miracle would change its fortunes. Its style was geared towards the blandness of agricultural shows in the *platteland* and charitable fêtes and cake sales in the 'proper' urban surburbs. The Nationalist Party Government called its bluff on every issue that had a semblance of political validity: racism, white domination, the rule of law, detention without trial, influx control and forced removals. Generally speaking, the response was in the vein: 'We understand why, but do you have to be so crude about it?'

But they faced, to be fair, a genuine political dilemma. To pose a clear alternative to the above problems was to expose them to a very real threat within the confines of white politics. As a party, it became vulnerable to attacks of selling out the white man, of ignoring the *swart gevaar* (black threat). As long as the name of the game was to pander to white prejudice, ignorance and fear within the limitations of white electoral politics, the old United Party acted properly although entirely ineffectively. Nobody, and no party until then, could outbid the Nationalist Party at this game. The United Party failed to see that the political risk that had to be taken by a white opposition in Parliament if it were to play a role, was to allow itself to become vulnerable in an attempt to broaden debate and focus attention on the central issues of political conflict.

Whatever its shortcomings, the Progressive Party and its successors tried to do that, particularly as regards issues of political, social and constitutional conflict. (I believe it should have done more on issues of economic conflict, but that is another matter.) No wonder then, that the most vicious attacks of *swart gevaar* politics and selling out to the black man against the Progressive Party came not only from the Nationalist Party but also from the United Party. And when this failed in the 1974 election with the seven seat breakthrough of the Progressive Party, the old United Party was caught in the classical dilemma of being eroded on two fronts that related to the contradiction in its centre: whether to outbid the Nationalist Party at its game or to go for a clearcut alternative. Soon after the 1974 election the cracks began to show.

First to break were a group of four members of Parliament under the leadership of Harry Schwarz. They represented the heart of the leadership of the so-called Young Turks movement that tried to create a more enlightened United Party. They became the Reform Party and negotiated a merger with the Progressive Party, which resulted in the formation of the Progressive Reform Party. Initially it was an uneasy alliance as there was no love lost between the reformists and some of the older members of the Progressive Party. They had fought each other in bitter electoral battles and unforgiveable things had been said.

Next, in what can only be described as an act of political hara-kiri, Sir De Villiers Graaff not only decided to retire (which was perfectly understandable as he had had a long innings), but also to disband the United Party and to form a new party called the New Republic Party which all 'fairminded and moderate' white South Africans were invited to join. The United Party promptly broke up in two predictable directions. John Wiley of Simonstown formed the South African Party with those who were the remnants of the old *bloedsap* contingent in the United Party, and they are now almost all members of the governing National Party (Wiley himself is a Cabinet Minister).

On the other hand, Japie Basson, Nic Olivier, Derek de Villiers, Harold van Hoogstraten and Senator Eric Winchester started negotiating with Eglin, and again a merger took place which resulted in the Progressive Federal Party. The old United Party had been reduced to a rump of its former self under the leadership of Cadman from Natal. He was the shortest reigning Leader of the official Opposition because shortly after these breakups and mergers, Prime Minister Vorster called a general election. He came back with the biggest majority ever for a Nationalist Party Prime Minister, but he also came back with a new official Opposition the 17-member Progressive Federal Party and its new Leader, Colin Eglin.

I think Eglin is one of the most underrated politicians in Parliament. He is tough, principled and a brilliant negotiator. Easily one of the most intelligent people I have met, he, unlike me, thrives on the traditions and activities of Parliament. In any normal democratic society Eglin would have been an invaluable member of the Government and such a Government could have counted itself privileged to have him. Through (I believe) very little fault of his own, his leadership battled along after the 1977 election. He could never count on the enthusiastic support of either Basson or Schwarz after the bruising mergers in which he, Eglin, had come out with most of the coups.

But even in the ranks of the old supporters of the 'Progs' rumblings were gathering momentum. I could never put them down to anything specific and assumed that they occurred because we were moving through the normal phases of a political party experiencing growth. In any case, I thought things would eventually settle down.

In the meantime the Information Scandal broke and had an earth-shattering impact on the traditional unity and leadership of the National Party. This period has been adequately documented in other publications. It is only relevant in this context in the sense that when the Government was reeling from its impact and should have been under constant pressure from the official Opposition, it managed to find a red herring to divert attack away from itself. One of the planks in Vorster's 1977 election campaign platform was blatant anti-Americanism in saying that the election was an opportunity for white South Africa to tell America we would not tolerate any interference in our internal affairs. The Carter Administration with its aggressive stance towards South African domestic policy had been effectively used by the Nationalist Party to consolidate electoral support against outside intervention rather than support for its own policies. But, the consequences in terms of votes cast remained the same. One person in paticular who was singled out for abuse and vilification in this anti-Carter hysteria was Don McHenry, the United States Ambassador to the United Nations who was personally known to Eglin.

In Parliament, Pik Botha, Minister of Foreign Affairs, an able debater who can combine melodrama and demagoguery with devastating effect, managed to load a private phone call of Eglin's to Don McHenry with such sinister significance that you could have sworn Eglin was up for high treason. I believe Eglin handled the attack badly. Instead of metaphorically leaping across the floor and kicking Botha into a heap in the back benches, he came across hesitant and uncertain, and a new political myth was born. Whereas we should have been rampant in our attack on the Government's handling of the Information Scandal, we found ourselves in the ridiculous situation of having to handle Eglin's entirely innocent phone call to McHenry. I have no doubt that this whole episode affected Eglin's leadership and the position of the party badly. However, I sincerely believed it would be a temporary setback.

These were the immediate political circumstances. When it became public knowledge that I had made myself available for the nomination of Principal of the University of Cape Town I was not prepared for the reaction in the party. There had been intermittent speculation and even requests that I should become Leader, but I always squashed them and said I was not interested. Now it was made clear to me that if I should leave politics some key figures in the party would do the same.

It is always difficult to judge a situation in the heat of the moment, but I judged those who held these views to be serious. My overriding feeling was that it would have been pointless to sacrifice the efforts of the last few years to form a new official opposition and to try and get a new debate going. I agreed to withdraw my nomination, but stated that I would not work against Eglin and would only be available to lead if he himself were no longer available, and then only for a limited time. Some were determined to bring about a situation in which Eglin would not be available. A special Federal Executive Meeting was called to discuss the leadership issue and I made it quite clear that I would not tolerate a motion of no-confidence in Eglin. In my view it was the last thing he deserved. However, I feared that if somebody moved a motion of confidence it could have the same effect. The night before the meeting Eglin and I spoke on the phone and I said I would certainly see to it, as far as possible, that a motion of no-confidence would not be put and urged him to persuade some others who might be willing not to put in a motion of confidence. I hoped that we could simply talk the meeting out and let the whole issue be overtaken by new political developments. It was not to be. The very first speech moved a motion of full confidence in Eglin. He lost and events were set in motion so that I became the Leader of the official Opposition at a party congress in November.

As I said, I did so with reluctance. Eglin personified dignity in the way he coped with a very hurtful period in his life as a public figure. I suspect he has never forgiven some of those who connived against him. Our own relationship went through a strained initial period, but has since settled down to one of bluntness devoid of pettiness. Whenever he has criticized me, and he has not hesitated when he felt it necessary, I have never suspected any ulterior motive. I feel that he would have done many things differently and no doubt better than I have done them, but he has never tried to impose his methods on me.

There followed a lonely period for me. The pressures of the new position and the increased tempo of my daily life did not leave much time for self-pity and personal reflection. The added tension of the new position had a worsening effect on my domestic situation. As far as the job itself was concerned, after a few initial hiccups, finding a secretary and settling into a new office, I knuckled down to it soon enough. The friendship and support of Gordon Waddell, Nic Olivier and Alex Boraine during this period was invaluable. Soon my first real test presented itself.

It ended with the expulsion of Japie Basson, one-time Deputy Chairman of the party and Chairman of the parliamentary caucus, from the caucus, and his resignation from the party.

As I mentioned, Eglin, Basson, Dalling and myself served on a parliamentary Commission of Inquiry to investigate the possibility of introducing a new constitution for the country. A few explanatory remarks are necessary to indicate the significance of such terms of reference for a white parliamentary Commission of Inquiry. Another Commission of Inquiry had been appointed under the Chairmanship of Professor Erika Theron to investigate the socio-economic and political position of the Coloured population. When the Report was tabled in 1976 its recommendations were a devastating indictment of the Government's policy towards the Coloured population. One of the recommendations of the Report was that a special commission should be appointed to investigate the 'direct political representation of Coloureds on all levels of Government'. This recommendation, in retrospect, precipitated a series of events which was to lead to the end of the last white Parliament in Africa. The reaction of the Government to this recommendation was to come forward with a set of constitutional proposals which envisaged three separate Parliaments, one each for Coloureds, Asians and whites, with a common Council of Cabinets. These were the so-called 'three Parliament' proposals and were duly processed through the National Party caucus and Provincial Congresses for approval. Only Cas Greyling, MP for Carletonville in the National Party caucus, objected and resigned. He was a crusty, tough old campaigner and I remember admiring his courage and integrity at the time. He was one of the first Nationalist MPs that spoke to me in a friendly manner when I got to Parliament in 1974. He had been in Parliament for more than two decades and one evening during the break he started talking to me in the parliamentary pub.

He remarked, 'I, Cas Greyling, don't say that Parliament needs Cas Greyling, but by God, Cas Greyling certainly needs Parliament!'

Prime Minister Vorster used these proposals as one of three reasons for calling the 1977 election, the other two being his anti-American non-interventionism and the need to find out who the real official opposition in the country was going to be. I have already mentioned that he received a massive mandate. However, he had no mandate from the constituencies that were supposed to be the primary beneficiaries of the new constitution, the so-called Coloureds and Indians. They either ignored it or vehemently rejected it. Soon afterwards Vorster retired to become State President and P W Botha succeeded Vorster. One of his problems was the 'three Parliament' set of proposals which the majority of whites, and in particular the Nationalist Party, had approved, but which nobody else wanted.

In politics, when in doubt create a commission. P W Botha announced a parliamentary Commission of Inquiry into the Constitution. The terms of reference were very wide indeed: 'To investigate the introduction of a new Constitution for the Republic of South Africa.' Botha referred the 'three Parliament' set of proposals to the Commission as evidence to be considered. It was an all-party commission and that is how Basson, Eglin, Dalling and myself found ourselves on it representing the PFP. A commission of this kind can serve a host of political purposes: its intention may be a genuine attempt to reach all-party consensus on a controversial issue, to depoliticize a matter; to postpone a difficult decision indefinitely; to play for time in the hope that some new development will provide a breakthrough to take the heat temporarily out of a touchy political issue before re-introducing it. We had no way of knowing what the hidden agenda was, but we certainly took a great deal of verbal and written evidence. Three things were common to the evidence almost without exception: the existing constitution was untenable; a new one could not be imposed by one group on any other and had to be negotiated; and no group of significance – racial, ethnic, or political – could be excluded from such negotiations. For us in the PFP this was old hat, but also exciting because it confirmed the constitutional process assumptions we were propagating at the time.

Consequently we were on the lookout for any sign of movement from the Government side because that was where it really mattered.

There is no doubt that Chris Heunis, the present Minister of Constitutional Affairs, was the moving force on that Commission and for that matter all subsequent constitutional developments. Many people find him arrogant, vain and intolerant and there is some validity to that, but he has a nimble mind, is a very tough, almost bullying negotiator and has a shrewd political instinct. It was always stimulating to engage him because he loved a good argument and was one of the few exceptions in Parliament who not only understood the rules of logic, but tried to honour them. It soon became apparent that Heunis wanted the Commission to deliver something and not just bubble away on some political back-burner. After months of taking evidence at various centres in the country, and when I had become Leader of the official Opposition, Heunis drew me aside during tea break at the Durban City Hall and said it was pointless to carry on hearing and reading evidence that essentially repeated the same points. He felt that some concrete recommendations should come from the Commission. He went on to say that he was thinking along the lines of a permanent multi racial constitutional body, but had not finalized his ideas.

I enthusiastically supported the general idea, and was genuinely excited. Not only did this indicate some development which we in the PFP believed to be necessary to get out of the constitutional cul-de-sac, but it was also quite certain that Heunis would not move in this direction without Cabinet backing. Heunis suggested that in subsequent meetings of the Commission we should try to identify areas of consensus, and this was certainly the general disposition of myself and the other members of the PFP on the Commission.

It soon became clear in the discussions of the Commission that we agreed on the three areas which the evidence appeared to emphasize: the existing constitution was untenable; a new one had to be negotiated and could not be unilaterally imposed by any group; and in such negotiation no population group could be excluded from participation. It was at a meeting of the Commission in the Provincial Council Building in Cape Town that I realized with deep dismay that the consensus was more apparent than real. Heunis beckoned me to come out of the hearings for a chat. We met in the office of the Administrator of the Cape. He said that he was going ahead with proposing the idea of a President's Council, but that blacks definitely could not be given status on such a Council equal to Coloureds and Asians and whites.

A separate black Council would have to be formed. I said that neither I nor my caucus would be able to support this, and I sensed we both felt unhappy that the issue was going to develop into a political scrap. The Commission brought out its report and the PFP attached its own minority report as part of it.

There is no doubt that some misunderstanding or confusion developed between Heunis and myself. I do not know who was responsible for it, maybe I was or one or two of my other colleagues on the Commission. Somehow Heunis did not expect the PFP and/or me to oppose the recommendations and subsequent legislation as strongly as we did. The issue was not only whether we opposed the composition of the President's Council but also whether we would serve on it. Nobody in the PFP caucus especially not the Chairman, Japie Basson, could have been in any doubt as to how I, or the overwhelming majority of the PFP caucus, felt about the President's Council and participation on it. It was clearly 'No' all along the way.

Therefore, there was consternation in our ranks when we read in the *Sunday Times* that Basson himself had said he was prepared to serve on the President's Council if he were asked. (This before we had publicly debated or finalized a caucus decision). Anyone who knows Parliament and the caucus system, knows this means trouble.

Privately I told Japie Basson that an untenable situation was developing and that he had to do something about it. He said he was an old enough hand at the game and would put things right in the debate itself. The matter was raised in the caucus again, and again he said he knew the consequences of going against the caucus decision and that he would put the matter right in the debate. I put our position quite clearly in the debate, opposing the Bill and stating unequivocally that we would not serve on the President's Council. But the press and especially the Government benches, who were now openly taunting me and the party, were waiting for Japie Basson to speak. The next day I sat expressionless as he repeated the contents of the *Sunday Times* article in his speech. In essence he appreciated the PFP caucus position and respected it, but if he were asked whether he would serve on the President's Council he would. This coming from the Chairman of the PFP caucus was totally against the rules of the game as everyone in Parliament knew them.

The funny thing is, I liked Japie Basson. I enjoyed talking to him: he is a serious student of politics and a mine of information on federal political systems. He knew white politics inside out and I enjoyed listening to his anecdotes on the subject during the many conversations we had. Besides, his son-in-law, Christo Wiese, had been with me as a student at Stellenbosch and we got on very well. In addition, my whole dispostion was anti-authoritarian and I hated making a fetish of convention simply for the sake of observing it. But his actions on the President's Council raised issues of deep political commitment in me. For some time I had sensed a parting of the ways developing between Japie Basson and me on these issues. The two central ones involved voluntary association in politics and the involvement of blacks in negotiating a political solution. Whatever other factors may have played a role – Japie Basson's own private agenda; the fact that I had just become the Leader and was under pressure to show how I would deal with it – all this was secondary to what I believed to be the role that a white opposition could play if it were to make a substantial contribution to political negotiations in the future. I do not deny that I was disappointed in the manner in which he had acted towards me personally, but I had been slighted and insulted by members of my caucus on other occasions without having to take action.

I did not sleep easily that night and early the next morning phoned him and explained that I was going to propose to caucus that the privileges of the Whips be withdrawn from him. It was all over by nine o'clock. Japie Basson is undoubtedly today still unhappy about what happened and often I run into little pools of bitterness against me and the party left by him in the social circuit, but I have not a moment's doubt that I acted correctly in the situation.

Publicly he was responsible for the 'boycott' image being tagged to the party. This is a false and superficial description but it is one of those spiteful epithets that cling in politics – a convenient way out of coping with a difficult argument. P W Botha, ever the Party politician with the eye for the gap, sensing that the boycott tag was running and wishing to promote the President's Council (and no doubt because he wanted his own mandate from the white electorate) called the 1981 General Election. Even sympathetic newspapers predicted that we

68

would be fortunate if we came back with the same number of seats that we held then.

I always remind myself at such times not to lose my perspective. A common misconception among South African parliamentary politicians is that they are at the centre of what is happening in the country and sometimes even the world. It is not difficult to fall into this trap. Whites, being the dominant minority, have used their position of power and privilege to create institutions which service a social, economic and political pecking order where a sense of self-importance is automatically reinforced. Many times I have gone to occasions where with great pomp and ceremony medals of merit are awarded, a boat is launched, an Honorary Doctorate is conferred, and when I look around at those assembled, I might as well be in a polite drawing room somewhere in Europe.

The speeches almost invariably define a universe of discourse which is exclusively European in its references, arrogant and presumptuous 'the country is grateful'; 'the people honour you'; 'your service to the community'; 'this is an extremely popular choice'. If you travel twenty kilometres into the nearest township the average resident will not have the vaguest idea who is being talked about and will no doubt reserve such sentences for sports heroes. In a fragmented society this is to be expected to some extent, but I feel that we have managed to make fragmentation the abiding virtue of our social order. Nowhere is this more in evidence than during a 'general election' in which the white political parties seek a 'democratic' mandate from the 'people'. How often has a Nationalist Prime Minister in the past, flushed with success and with becoming humility, thanked God for the trust that the people have put in him to lead them for the next few years.

For me, the excitement of such an election lay in the extent to which we could broaden awareness in the white electorate by questioning the conventional assumptions of parliamentary politics – a risky business, because as a party you become so vulnerable to attacks from your opponents.

But for me the relevance of white opposition politics lay in putting the case for broadening political participation to all groups in society without decreasing my party's support in white politics and perhaps even increasing it. As this becomes more possible the variability in the exercise of political power increases, and this I believe to be a pre-condition for negotiation politics to work. Without voluntary white co-operation evolutionary change is impossible.

That is why the 1981 election was a high risk one for us in the official Opposition. We had rejected the President's Council as being racist and inadequate as a negotiating instrument. The PFP opposed it because it excluded blacks. This refrain was either going to gain legitimacy in white politics or we would be wiped out. Against the background of post-colonial disintegration of stable governments all around us it was a bumpy political road to travel. One recurring theme of attack against us was: 'look at Mozambique, Angola', and 'you want Lancaster House for South Africa'; (the latter of course referred to developments in Zimbabwe). There is no tougher customer than a white Rhodesian who refused to adjust in his own country, came to South Africa long before settlement in Rhodesia and who whips up racial animosity here.

Through their actions here many ex-Rhodesians create the very conditions which led them to leave their own country in the first place. I often thought of Santayana's phrase: 'those who do not learn from the mistakes of history, are doomed to repeat them'.

On a personal level I worked until fatigue was a sore in the pit of my stomach. I was unopposed in my own constituency and free to campaign elsewhere. Averaging three to four meetings a day, I talked and talked until I could not stand the sound of the words coming out of my mouth. Travelling around the country I looked forward to a few hours of anonymity and total acceptance at some of my favourite watering holes: a room at Schlemmer's house in Durban where I would arrive late at night, listen to music and have a glass of wine; the home of my sister, Marcia, always warm with mother earth generosity; or those of Ian MacDonald, Gordon Waddell and Kathy, and Max Borkum. Most of the time I would end the day in some hotel room listening to the late news on the radio.

We were lucky too. There were three and even four-cornered fights that gave us chances where none had existed. The New Republic Party was on the retreat in Natal. Some Cabinet Ministers had made some unbelievable campaign statements. First prize went to 'Lapa' Munnik, Minister of Health at the time who stated and repeated that old age pensioners could eat enough on R20 per month.

The Prime Minister had not yet changed his campaign style and came across as his old belligerent, abusive and alienating self. And so on. When the shouting was over we had not only held our own seats but gained eight new ones.

In my own way I had also been given a mandate and felt vindicated in what I had done. It is not moral vindication you seek; that you have to resolve long before, when issues of strategy and principle are decided. I have a dogged belief that it is not necessary to hoodwink, bluff or play hidden agenda politics with the electorate. In fact, I believe it is counter productive. Of course, expediency is part of political mobilization but it is dangerous to think that you can indefinitely do 'clever things with a stupid electorate' and get away with it, or deliberately misinform them to gain their support to do things they may not support. Whatever the reasons people voted for the PFP in 1981 (and these may be numerous, fickle and even unrelated to those I hoped they had voted for) I felt satisfied that I had not pulled any punches or misled them about the difficulties which lay ahead. I also learned a simple maxim of political leadership which has been confirmed many times since: the quality and extent of praise or blame for your leadership is unrelated to your intentions. Historical coincidence is perhaps a more important ingredient for greatness than ability.

Whatever your fortunes, it is a mistake to think that you can take charge of the future, and also to take yourself too seriously.

Black exclusion – white folly

You soon realize that an important part of political energy is devoted to distorting the intentions of your opponent; to exaggerating the consequences of his policy alternative to your own and to caricaturing his fundamental assumptions. In Parliament this serves two basic purposes: it helps to avoid a real debate on any issue and it lends an artificial validity to one's own position in the sense that, 'if his options are so bad, mine must be better'. In this way nonsense, hyperbole and good old-fashioned bullshit become an essential part of the ritual of Parliament. All sides partake in this ritual and if you listen long enough, it cures insomnia.

One such distortion which has persisted for as long as I have been in Parliament is that we in the PFP are the remnants of 19th century liberalism; a political anachronism that refuses to come to terms with decolonization and the 'realities' of Third World politics. In the hustings this finds expression in election language such as our being 'mink and manure' liberals who can buy their apartheid and 'bleeding hearts who lean over blackwards on every issue'. This vituperation is triggered by our insistence that it is the white man's folly to think that he can find long-term political stability by excluding blacks from a commonly agreed upon constitutional arrangement. I do not deny that in advancing this accusation South African liberals have played an important part in presenting and popularizing some good, bad and indifferent arguments.

Naturally their opponents have seized upon the bad and indifferent ones because of the intellectual and especially moral discomfort caused by the good ones.

In the popular political sense South African liberalism has three main components that have their well-argued roots in liberal philosophy, whether of the 19th or 20th century variety. There is *political* liberalism with its emphasis on 'one man, one vote' and unrestrained majoritarianism in decision-taking. Universal adult suffrage has become one of the defining qualities of democratic political systems in the world, but the insistence that majority rule is its inevitable corollary could in certain circumstances lead to severely undemocratic consequences. I believe South Africa presents one of those circumstances. *Economic* liberalism finds its expression in the free enterprise ethic, a belief that if the factors of production are unrestrainedly combined in the pursuit of profit the greatest economic benefit for all would result. Political liberalism can have some profoundly negative consequences for economic liberalism, particularly if an unbridled majority interferes with the so-called market forces in the exercise of political power. *Social* liberalism has focused attention on individual human rights or civil liberties: the rule of law, freedom of speech, of association and of organization.

It would be uncommon to find political and economic liberals who are not social liberals as well, but it is possible to find social liberals who are not economic or political liberals, such as someone who believes deeply in civil liberties but not in majority rule and/or unrestrained free enterprise. Again, the PFP and its predecessors have been strong on social liberalism, slightly less strong on economic liberalism and quite weak on political liberalism.

Take *political* liberalism. The old Progressive Party had a qualified franchise as part of the policy, something I found personally unacceptable as it smacked of élitism and paternalism and was based on erroneous generalizations about political participation. The old Progs tried to manoeuvre with the franchise part of political liberalism and to leave the decision-taking part (majority rule) alone. I on the other hand, believe the franchise is the good part of political liberalism and the decision-taking part the bad. That is why the current PFP policy proposals focus on the problem of political decision-taking and domination. In that sense I am not a conventional political liberal. I do not believe that majority rule in decision-taking is a precondition for good democratic government.

Again, when it comes to economic liberalism I have certain reservations. I certainly believe in free enterprise, but if it has no restraint whatsoever, certain social conditions can arise which will have political consequences profoundly detrimental to any free enterprise at all. Therefore the political system must be of such a kind that it can allow those who govern to anticipate and prevent those social conditions from reaching such negative proportions. Here I have in mind particularly the welfare of the aged, the sick, the young and the destitute as well as the provision of such essential services which free enterprise is not able or willing to provide. I also believe in the right of labour to organize and to bargain. In this sense I suppose I am not an economic liberal.

Therefore, to call the official Opposition in the last white Parliament in Africa liberals is not only to distort the political picture but to do an injustice to South African liberalism in general. Political liberals of the pure variety look down their noses at us for being soft on majority rule. In any case, as a political movement or party they voluntarily disbanded with the introduction of the Political Interference Act. If a head count had to be taken among economic liberals with considerable financial clout, such as big business, it would not surprise me one bit if the vast majority of them quietly tuck in behind the power of the Government.

In any case, they donate far more money to the Nationalist Party than to the Progressive Federal Party and I know what I am talking about. They are wary of the PFP generally and suspect us of being closet political liberals who, should we come to power, would create political instability which is bad for business. Both economic liberals, out of a sense of guilt perhaps, and political liberals, patronizingly approve of our stand on civil liberties. But all these distinctions are immediately squashed out of existence in the hustings. All the characteristics of liberalism South African style are distorted, exaggerated and inflated for the purposes of competition in the white political arena, and the last white Parliament ended with us still being called 'Hoggenheimers', 'fat cats' (economic liberals), 'proponents of black majority rule', 'sell-outs' (political liberals) or 'romantics' and 'idealists' on human rights (social liberals). And these attacks were completely interchangeable and unrelated. If they could not cope with our human rights position, they would use a majority rule attack, and vice versa. If I had to use clichés to depict the last official Opposition in the last white Parliament based on a certain consistency that revealed itself in debates on votes and Bills, I would say that politically it was conservative (in the philosophical sense), economically it was social democrat and socially it was liberal.

The social attack of South African liberalism on apartheid and separate development is devastating and unanswerable and I am proud to be associated with it. Its values lie at the heart of my own rejection of such racist laws as the Population Registration Act and others dependent on its implementation. But I certainly do not have to accept all the tenets of political and economic liberalism to argue why black constitutional exclusion is the white man's folly. In other words, it is shortsighted to dismiss all arguments against black exclusion as liberal ravings, and I believe there are some in Government who are beginning to realize this.

I find it convenient to distinguish between two justifications of separate development/apartheid. One has to do with simple racial segregation – strictly speaking the apartheid leg of separate development. Here segregationary measures such as the Population Registration Act, the Group Areas Act, the Separate Amenities Act, come to mind. The crudest racist justifications dressed up in quasi-theological gobbledy-gook characterized this period of political development (a learned Professor who taught me theology actually wrote an article entitled: 'Apartheid, the Will of God'). It is encouraging to see more and more Afrikaans academics ridiculing this kind of political clap-trap.

The other justification has to do with black political exclusion – the separate development leg of apartheid. Whereas apartheid rationalizations began to take shape almost immediately after 1948, separate development rationalizations began to take shape from 1960 onwards when the homelands concept came into being. This was the beginning of Verwoerdian apartheid which depended on, but was not the same as, Malan-Strydom apartheid. The rationalizations for the one shaded into those for the other, but the two differed markedly in intellectual quality and logical coherence. Separate development rationalizations depended on the social ordering brought about by enforced segregation by means of the original apartheid measures. The outstanding characteristic was the destruction of voluntary association. On this structure of involuntary association further involuntary associations could be imposed for the purposes of constitutional development, and thus the peculiar concept of ethnicity/tribality/group identity by which separate development operates, was born.

As I have said, South African liberalism is devastating in its critique of apartheid structures. It has been weaker in its attack on separate development structures.

Whatever else can be said about separate development – Verwoerdian apartheid – as an ideology, it has a coherence and systemic quality which cannot be dismissed as racism pure and simple. It has been profoundly racist in its consequences for the people who suffered from its implementation, but as an ideological package it has had intellectual appeal which managed to morally seduce more than the ignorant and unreflective racists in our society. Come to think of it, it was the first new and coherent post-colonial era response to the political, social and economic difficulties generated by decades of colonial exploitation. The standard reaction of the colonizing countries to these difficulties was either to get out, with dignity and pomp if possible, or to impose first some hastily concocted constitutional package which saved their faces if not the countries they were deserting. Separate development had an indigenous, post-colonial look about it, and it was an ideological response by whites to a colonial situation which they would not and could not leave. Political liberalism's critique of it and its alternative of one-man-one-vote-majority-rule sounded alien by comparison. This was, initially, also the case with the critique of economic liberalism which appeared to promise nirvana if only the unrestrained benefits of free enterprise were allowed to soothe the aches of the colonial inheritance.

Now, of course, under the protection of state and monopoly capitalism a new generation of Afrikaner economists is emerging, behaving as if free enterprise is the best thing since sliced bread and as if they invented it.

But, and this is really the point I wish to make, you do not have to depend on the assumption of political and economic liberalism to knock the stuffing out of separate development as an ideology. I was a student at Stellenbosch at the beginning of the Sixties when it was being articulated. I remember the excitement, even thrill, some experienced when it was explained for the first time. Any aware young Afrikaner knew instinctively and with a pervading sense of doom that apartheid until then was a holding action, that a solution to living with the blacks still had to be found. Here, some sensed, was the beginning of one. It made logical sense and addressed very prickly moral issues. The beauty of it was the audacity of its most basic assumptions 'You don't have to find a solution to living with blacks, because there are no blacks, only ethnic groups who cannot really tolerate one another anyway. Therefore, You have to separate these groups from one another and let them develop along their own lines. Thus, separate development! Come to think of it, if You let them develop far enough they will actually come to realize that they are really foreigners in South Africa and belong to independent countries.

You, as whites, do not have a problem with blacks, you have a problem with foreigners in your own country. But so do many other countries', and so on and so on. This sounds like a caricature. Yet twenty-five years later in the last session of the last white Parliament, there was not one Nationalist MP who would have had the courage to deny that these were still the basic assumptions of separate development, even though the social, economic and political realities around them howled out the contradictions.

Notice above, how I used the word You. I call it the royal You. It always sneaks into the political analysis of those who suffer from delusions of grandeur about their ability to take charge of history, the present and the future, and control all three. Separate development says that You solve the problem by excluding it from the solution. Exclusion is the solution! When I opposed the President's Council for the first time, they (Nationalists) turned on me and said – 'But blacks are excluded because "adequate provision has already been made for them!"' When I opposed the new constitution because of black exclusion, they said 'But their constitutional solution is progressing along a different path!' Exclusion is the solution! That is why, apart from anything else, separate development is the most costly and grandiose political demonstration of one of the simplest lessons of life: you can never solve a problem by pretending it does not exist. And that is why black exclusion is the white man's folly in the land of their common heritage and birth.

Of course it is a bit more complicated than this. Those who conceived of separate development were not consciously pretending the problem did not exist. (Although many of their present followers do.) On the contrary, they thought they were devoting all their skills to solving it. As in all durable political ideologies some truths are accommodated within its core assumptions. It would be equally short sighted to ignore these truths when attacking separate development and its consequences for South Africa. In a country with population characteristics such as ours, patterns of inter-racial and inter-ethnic interaction stubbornly persevere and cannot be explained away as manifestations of mysticism. We are far enough into the post-colonial era to know these patterns are complicated by, but certainly not solely attributable to, white domination, capitalism or colonialism. Therefore it is irresponsible to look for political solutions as if these patterns do not exist. It would be self-defeating to try to undo the consequences of separate development by repeating its central mistake, that is, ignoring the very problem you wish to solve. To avoid this we must examine how the basic mistake of separate development was implemented.

The factual part on which separate development is based is the existence of various tribal or ethnic communities in South Africa. That there are such groups cannot be denied.

However this fact was seized upon almost to the exclusion of all other facts as the basis for a constitutional framework within which a black person, as a member of an ethnic or tribal community, had to pursue his political aspirations. Laws were passed by a white Parliament which compelled a black person to exercise his political rights within the ethnic or tribal political institutions created by the white Parliament.

Given the above the legend of separate development goes as follows:

South Africa consists of a plurality of ethnic minorities. Ethnic loyalties and group identities are so strong and competitive that they cannot be adequately accommodated within a common political or constitutional framework. Therefore separate territories with their own political institutions have to be developed so that these minorities can live out their separate and conflicting political aspirations.

Only in this way will inter-racial and inter-ethnic political conflict be avoided and stability be ensured. To put this legend into practice the following steps were envisaged:

Land areas were identified as constituting the tribal homelands of the various ethnic groups, the so-called Native Trust areas that had been legislatively set aside in 1913 and 1936. Not by the wildest stretch of the imagination were they initially seen as constituting the geography of independent national states.

Nevertheless, once these areas had been established, they were given self-governing status and legislative assemblies were created for them.

The final stages of constitutional independence could be reached by any of these legislative assemblies asking for sovereign independence. So far, four such states have come into being: Transkei, Venda, Bophuthatswana and Ciskei. The hope is that eventually all the remaining homeland areas will be independent in this fashion.

As each homeland achieves 'independence' its citizens lose their South African citizenship and become foreigners. Therefore, in a real sense the Separate Development Homeland Independence policy is part of a process of massive denationalization of the majority of the people of South Africa.

But the determination of the Government to convert this ideological legend into political reality has created the following problems:

1. There is not enough land to accommodate physically the people supposed to be citizens of the homelands. Just under 13% of the total land surface is set aside for the envisaged independent nation states which will become the constitutional and political home of 75% of the people of South Africa.

2. Even if all the homelands are consolidated according to the 1975 proposals they will not constitute undivided units of territory. Most of them will consist of several pieces of land thus creating major problems concerned with the administration of 'international' boundaries.

3. In all cases, the vast majority of the citizens of these homelands and 'independent states' live and work outside them. Many of them have never been there or do not even know what they look like. The Government has reluctantly conceded the permanence of blacks outside the homelands after more than twenty-five years of trying to implement separate development.

4. The homelands and 'independent states' almost without exception are financially heavily dependent on the South African Government and economy and certainly have no economic viability of their own. Without economic assistance from the South African Government and migrant worker wages flowing

79

back to the homelands and independent states they would suffer immediate economic collapse.

5. The so-called 'independent states' enjoy no international recognition whatsoever and are recognized as sovereign only by one another and by the South African Government.

6. As in most Third World regions where conditions of prolonged stable poverty exist, there is a very high birth rate in the homelands and 'independent states', coupled with malnutrition, hunger and the depletion of natural resources.

7. The independent homelands policy has in no way weakened the insistence of the vast majority of black South Africans that they are still citizens of South Africa. Nor has international pressure slackened in this regard. In fact this insistence is, if anything, stronger than ever.

8. The policy has failed to engender a sense of identification on the part of urban blacks with the homeland governments or areas. Consequently such governments lack legitimacy in their eyes and this makes it very difficult to create viable political structures in the urban areas if such structures are linked to the policy of creating independent homelands.

9. Because of increasing rural poverty, drought and unemployment as well as industrialization, black urbanization is gathering a momentum that shifts attention away from constitutional development in the rural areas to the inevitable problems of urban conflict.

10. The focus on 'homeland independence' and separate ethnic development has been accompanied by neglect of any systematic policy to cope with urbanization. In fact, for a long time it was assumed that the flow to the cities would weaken and that black urbanization would taper off.

Now there is an awakening to this problem, and the more the awareness grows of the need for such a policy, the clearer it becomes that the fundamental assumptions of separate development are ludicrous.

Despite these problems the Government persisted in persuing the fundamental objective of separate development, which is to bring about a situation where constitutionally there will be no black South Africans. Some disastrous consequences have resulted:

1. The policy has immeasurably aggravated the poverty and deprivation of the rural homelands not only by trying to prevent the exodus of blacks who wished to seek work elsewhere, but also by adding to their numbers through a system of massive forced removal of whole communities and relocation of people resident outside the homelands into the homelands.

2. Overcrowding of these areas has systematically destroyed and wasted their agricultural potential and natural resources. They are now even less able to sustain human life than before. The irony is that a policy which was supposed to stimulate a drift to the rural areas has instead intensified the process of urban migration.

3. To regulate the drift to metropolitan areas a system of influx control has been developed – a complex of laws and regulations premised on the assumption that eventually no blacks will be South African citizens. Accordingly, the temporary nature of their sojourn outside the homeland area is underscored. Thus, no black may be in an urban area for longer than seventy-two hours without a permit, a migrant labourer may not have his family with him whilst he works in an area outside the homeland and he must return there once a year for a month; no black may own residential or any other property outside the homeland area. Hundreds of thousands of blacks are prosecuted for contravening these pass laws. Government is now reconsidering this policy.

4. The homelands policy and influx control has for a long time created the dangerous illusion that the problem of urban migration is being controlled, which in turn has led to the neglect on a massive scale of the urban living conditions of blacks. Inadequate land has been set aside for residential planning; an inadequate housing policy increased the backlog; townships were created more as sleep-in dormitories on the outskirts of towns and cities than as viable, self-sustaining communities; no significant commercial or trading rights were allowed. Because of influx control these townships are overcrowded and it is virtually impossible to get an exact census of the number of inhabitants. For example, two years ago the official figure for Soweto was 780 000 people whereas it was commonly accepted as being closer to 2 million.

5. The pressure of urban migration and unsystematic urban planning has seen the development of 'illegal' squatting on an ever-increasing scale. Raids, demolitions and relocation have become the order of the day, under the futile injunction that 'they have to go back where they came from'. And problems of emergency housing and squatting are going to intensify not ease off.

6. Consequently, land has been institutionalized as one of the major issues of racial competition in South Africa. The over-crowding of the homelands and the urban black communities has underscored the fact that the physical accommodation of racial groups is becoming one of the key issues of conflict in South Africa. It is common for whites to talk about 'white South Africa' and 'black homelands', about 'black townships' outside 'white cities'. Yet any one of them can stand in the main street of any major city at noon on any work-day and see how absurd such notions are.

7. It is always difficult to calculate precisely the return on investment of public expenditure, as much of it involves intangibles such as health, welfare, and education. But whatever criteria are used in assessing the 'profitability' of separate homeland development, measured against the stated objectives or goals of the policy, there is very little return on investment, only an exploding financial liability. Bureaucratic empires have been multiplied in the rural areas, which in most cases service the aspirations of self-sustaining privileged élites in deserts of poverty and malnutrition. With a few honourable exceptions, the leadership in many instances reinforces the racial stereotypes colonials held of blacks' ability to govern or administer. This perpetuates the prejudice that 'you cannot trust them with a thing' and makes the development of a more democratic political system even more difficult.

8. Cost must also be calculated in other areas: duplication of facilities in education, health, welfare; administering influx control and creating job opportunities in rural areas through failed decentralization policies such as 'border industrial development' where considerable inducements were offered to industrialists to establish industries on the borders of homeland areas. Of course, any acceptable solution or settlement to our problem is

going to involve financial expenditure on an enormous scale. But separate development is not acceptable or viable and therefore a waste of money and resources.

9. Perhaps the most disastrous consequence of the policy is the incalculable damage it has done to the average white and black psyche. It has smothered the initiative of human beings to do something for themselves – the State is expected to provide, regulate and control the individual's life. This has been anyway one of the most burdensome legacies of colonialism for socio-economic and political development. The highest good was to become a petty bureaucrat and wait for things to happen for you. Because the colonial masters monopolized the economy and the administration and the indigenous people were selectively incorporated to service the menial tasks, the most esteemed position in the post-colonial era was to become an administrator of some kind or other and to be paid for doing very little. With separate development we have gone further than that. Blacks are literally told where they *must* move, eat, sleep, work, go to school and relax. There is hardly a normal human activity that has not been legislatively proscribed. Consequently the black man knows the policy of separate development inside out, whereas the white is largely ignorant of its negative consequences and amongst whites who govern, it is largely confined to the grandiose underlying ideological assumptions of the policy. Is it surprising that there is a growing conviction amongst blacks that the only way there is going to be a 'chicken in every pot' is to be in charge of the political system and to dominate it with an alternative collectivist ideology?

10. So many consequences of separate development have been documented in disturbing detail that for my purposes it is not necessary to repeat them. Overall a major consequence has been to racialize almost all levels of interaction between black and white. Black/white polarization is stronger than ever in the history of this country. The more separate development has attempted to exclude blacks from the political system of South Africa, the more blacks have impinged socially and economically on the lives of whites. We are now more interdependent than ever before and at the same time black and white are

emotionally more apart also. Because of this, the conflict between us has become much more difficult to resolve.

But, one may ask, are those who conceived of this policy and those
who subsequently assisted in its implementation not aware of these
consequences? Is is possible, given the urgency of the times and the
difficulties which are obvious, that they stubbornly intend to persist in
such folly? One of the encouraging developments over the last decade
has been that academics and experts from within the governing establishment have begun to re-examine the consequences of the policy of
separate development and to question its fundamental assumptions.

From whichever perspective – economically, democratically, agri-
culturally, ecologically, in terms of the exigencies of economic
growth, community development, educational needs, conflict resolution, the creation of political legitimacy and leadership – the policy
has been torn to shreds and exposed. Even from those who govern in
Parliament such noises have been heard more frequently recently:
you are not inevitably a liberal if you question separate development
as a policy. In fact, the most devastating critique of it comes from applying its own assumptions to its consequences. It destroys itself by its
own logic.

That is why there have been changes which contradict the very
goals the policy set out to achieve. For example:
– a system of 99-year leasehold for property accepts the permanence
  of blacks in areas outside the homelands, *but* the absence of freehold highlights the reluctance with which this is done. Now even
  limited freehold is being offered.
– The homelands can never be fully consolidated and the system of
  consolidation persued thus far is costly and unproductive. *But*
  some other form of consolidation is being investigated rather than
  abandoning the idea itself.
– The present system of influx control is unacceptable, unworkable
  and a source of political instability and conflict. *But* a commission
  is investigating how to give it a kinder face rather than looking for
  an alternative.
– New strategies for industrial decentralization and deconcentration
  of industries are being pursued along more rational economic
  lines. *But* they fail to accept that we are not yet an over-urbanized

84

society exploiting the potential of our existing metropolitan centres and decentralization and deconcentration is no substitute for a rational policy of planned urbanization.

– Constitutional developments that have taken place for blacks in the urban areas are inadequate and ineffective. A Cabinet Committee has been appointed to examine this, *but* indications are that such examinations will regard the existence of homeland Governments as a fixed premise.

These adjustments have the potential to hasten the final collapse of the policy of separate development as initially conceived, and therein lies the hope for future developments. But I believe the reason the Government refuses to abandon the central assumptions of the policy is because it cannot acknowledge the fundamental lie or mistake which lies at the heart of it. What is it? If South Africa is a plurality of ethnic minorities that do not want to mix, that want to live separately and pursue different group interests, then laws that force or compel them to do so are a fundamental contradiction of that fact. If they want to do so, they will do so voluntarily. Why do black ethnic minorities need such laws, when white minorities do not? Does a Zulu need legal compulsion to be Zulu, but an Afrikaner, Jew or Portuguese can do so voluntarily?

Separate development cannot function without absurd laws. The core assumption of separate development – that this country contains a plurality of voluntary ethnic minorities – depends on laws which give the lie to that assumption.

That is its central mistake. It is here that the rationalization of apartheid/separate development meet and become an extension of each other. First, apartheid destroys voluntary association on a racial basis, then separate development attempts to do so on an ethnic basis. Nothing illustrates the untenability of separate development more vividly than the Government's actions towards black organizations which deliberately flouted the Government's policy of ethnic diversity. Is it surprising that with the onset of separate development in the sixties we also experienced the most brutally repressive security legislation in the history of the country? Verwoerd was an ideologue with dogmatic confidence. 'There are no blacks as such, only black ethnic minorities who wish to be apart'. Vorster was the policeman who not only saw to it that they stayed apart, but was determined to stamp out any attempt to establish unity amongst them. And as more and more coercion was applied to give effect to the lie of separate development, the crises of leadership and legitimacy deepened in the very institutions created to parade the lie. Underground, banned organizations became more fashionable, as well as counter-ideologies with a universal collectivist appeal. Thus was born the romance of 'the struggle', the 'will of the people', 'liberation', 'unity', 'Black Power', 'African socialism', 'real leaders' and the negative obverse of 'collaborators', 'stooges', 'part of the system'.

Nothing has brought about strategic solidarity amongst those who experience repression more strongly than the policy of separate development. This is its final failure. The situation brought about by separate development is simply that the diversity and support of the real political groupings amongst blacks are distorted and ambiguous because the Government insists that it will only deal with the artificial ones it has itself created.

The popular wisdom during Vorster's premiership was 'First let us settle the black issue then we will get to the Coloureds and Indians'. During the referendum in 1983 I shared a public platform with a Nationalist MP. When I argued the folly of black exclusion from the new Constitution he said to me, 'First let us settle the Coloured and Indian problem, then we will get to the blacks'. I suppose I must accept this as sign of hope, but, my God, what an admission after thirty-five years of separate development! Who have they been getting at all the time?

Interludes

Friendships continue to bring interludes of sanity and understanding. I am fortunate in the quality of friendships I have shared. Even those that have not endured with the intensity with which they were initially experienced, I recall with warmth. Some of them continue to shape my reaction to political experiences. It would be difficult to understand my own attitude to the demise of the last white Parliament without taking these friendships into account.

I have made many acquaintances in politics, but very few lasting intimate friends such as I had in academic life. Gordon and Kathy Waddell are valued exceptions. He and I were backbenchers together – a principled, straightforward man, uncomfortable in most social circumstances, and I learned to value his counsel on many important decisions that confronted me.

The first real by-election we fought as the old Progressive Party was A S K Pitman's in Durban North in 1976. Alex Boraine's was too soon after the General Election to stand out in my memory as a by-election, although we only won that one by thirty-four votes, and that in itself was something.

A few minutes after meeting each other Pitman and I recognized each other as kindred spirits. He was a passionate man who lived in a rage as if everything should have happened yesterday and today was only there to find out why not. When he laughed it seemed as if one looked right past his epiglottis into his heart, and he loved his own anecdotes and jokes even more than those who heard them for the first time. Most of them he told at his own expense. He fathered six beautiful children, was a successful and controversial advocate; farmed in a manner that defied all agricultural convention and was an erratic and frequently absent member of the House of Assembly. His speeches ranged from the devastatingly incisive to the incoherent. He was unimpressed with titles, power, pomp and ceremony and he detested all sham, self-indulgence and pretence. His world was peopled with either heroes or scoundrels whose actions affected the lives of ordinary people with whom he identified easily. He believed in certain ethical principles with an intensity matched only by the honesty with which he confessed his own inability to live up to them.

Whenever I am filled with a sense of impotent outrage at what is going on in politics and in my country, I think of Pitman. How we used to rage together and laugh at our impotence. I remember sitting in his chambers in Pietermaritzburg reading through the letters of young blacks who had left the country after the 1976 riots to join the 'liberation' struggle or simply to get out. The letters were from all over the world and were to their loved ones in Soweto and other black townships. They formed part of the evidence for the prosecution in a trial under the Terrorism Act in which Pitman was part of the counsel for the defence. I was struck by the realization of how ignorant the average white was of the fact that the relatives of those who were committed to the armed struggle, to violence, were living in our midst, working in our kitchens, gardens and factories and how futile it was for the Government to convince blacks that we were the subjects of some foreign 'total onslaught'. In fact, such a propaganda effort simply served to wrap whites into a tighter cocoon of ignorance and make them less prepared to meet the challenges that lay ahead. It was such a familiar pattern in the anti-colonial struggle; except that here in South Africa, the difference is that whites are not going to have the psychological escape of somewhere else to go.

Those Terrorism Act trials were for Pitman his real political experience, not Parliament. In those trials ideas concerning the futility of the struggle were stripped of rhetorical nonsense. They represented for him the crossroads where naked violence sought either to change or maintain the status quo and he found both indefensible.

But he could narrate those courtroom scenes with a dramatic authenticity that made your scalp tingle: the SASO nine coming up from the cells into the docks; clenched fists raised; their backs to the Bench, the gallery standing; returning the salute and singing 'Nkosi Sikelel' Afrika'; the judge ordering the court to be cleared; police lining the walls of the courtroom armed with machine pistols taking down the names of those who filed out. Two courtrooms away Breyten Breytenbach was being tried again for allegedly trying to escape. In Pitman's court Rick Turner was sitting waiting to give expert evi-

With my twin sister and her boyfriend. We were Head boy and Head girl at Pietersburg High School in 1958.

Top left:
With Colin Eglin, Flashgat *Ukaegbu* and Mr A D Blankson in Nigeria.

Bottom left:
Unexpected election night victory, Rondebosch, 1974. 'Sweet suffering grace,' I thought, 'what am I going to do now?'

Above:
With Alex Boraine investigating conditions at Crossroads squatter camp.

Top left:
'What's this place called?' I asked this squatter. 'Lourdes Farm,' he said. 'You know, Master, like the place of the Holy water.'

Bottom left:
Listening to the grievances of squatters at the 'KTC' camp in Nyanga East. With me are Reverend David Russell and an interpreter.

Above:
Mobbed by ecstatic supporters after the PFP victory in the Edenvale by-election in November, 1979, one of the most hotly contested by-elections in South Africa's history.

Above:
First visit to Maggie Thatcher with Dawie de Villiers, then Ambassador to the Court of St James, 1980.

Top right:
With Harry Pitman. His death punched a hole right through me.

Bottom right:
With Colin Eglin, a tough negotiator and top drawer politician.

With Mike Savage and David Welsh at the inauguration of my new study after the old one was gutted by a bomb blast.

After dinner speaker at the Amateur Road Runners' Association. It was the only way I could meet Bruce Fordyce (2nd back right) – I certainly didn't see him on the road when I ran with him.

With my wife Jane and my friend Nic Olivier.

With Harry Oppenheimer on the way to a lunch he hosted in a futile attempt to persuade the guests to vote No in the referendum.

Voting No in the referendum, 2 November 1983.

Receiving a gift in Ulundi from Mangosutho Buthelezi (left) after addressing the Kwazulu Legislative Assembly. King Goodwill Zwelithini is on my right.

Sir Lourens van der Post, myself and a Bobby on the way to 10 Downing Street for an interview with Maggie Thatcher, November 1984.

Three Afrikaners covering the white political spectrum: Botha (NP), Slabbert (PFP) and Treurnicht (CP).

Some senior Nationalist MPs look sceptical while PFP members are sworn into the first tri-cameral Parliament.

Debating against isolating South Africa at the Oxford Union, March 1985.

P W Botha remains a political enigma, a mixture of sentimentality and intolerance.

Nobel Peace Prize winner, Bishop Desmond Tutu.

Running in the Peninsula Marathon with Mike Tarr, MP for Pietermaritzburg North.

dence for the defence. He was murdered a few months later. 'Chee-rist,' Pitman would shout 'we are all stark raving crazy!' Even now, at six o'clock in the afternoon when Parliament is in Session, I have to restrain myself from looking back and giving him the wink for a few in the pub to ease the day. His death punched a hole right through me.

Charley Wiggin epitomizes one simple truth with which I have always had to come to terms – the futility of trying to opt out of a situation in which you remain intellectually, emotionally and morally involved. So far I have not been able to opt out; but I always remain tempted. Charley simply refuses to give up trying.

John Boorman is a film director who made the movie *Deliverance*. In the Summer School of the University of Cape Town in 1976 he gave a series of talks on his films and I met him. It was one of those meetings where we both knew it was unlikely that we were going to see each other again, but enjoyed each other's company sufficiently to prolong our discussions way beyond our initial intentions. I told him that I was due to visit the USA and Boorman insisted I see Lee Marvin, John Voigt and Burt Reynolds, who, he assured me, would make time if I mentioned his name. Also he said, if I had time, I should see a Charles Wiggin who was a technical adviser in the making of *Deliverance* (he apparently taught Voigt and Reynolds to canoe and swim the Appallachian Rapids) and was eccentric and interesting. I wrote to them all, but only Charley Wiggin responded, saying that he was not interested in meeting me; the others did not reply. Just before I departed he wrote again apologizing for his bluntness and said he would be happy to receive me. We became good friends. He is a medically retired lieutenant from the US marines and lives the life of gentleman farmer on a small holding in Fortson, Georgia, on a reasonable family inheritance.

He spends his day consuming energy (he eats non-stop), and (being a fitness fanatic) expending it with machine-like precision. In between he succumbs to brief little 'sinkers' (snoozes) and talks about the 'Los Angelization of America', 'big money – cash culture'; the viciousness of 'Southern pettiness and ignorance' the 'mechanization of meaning and experience' and the never-ending quest for Eldorado – somewhere on planet Earth where things must still be different. He has been to many places, but he always returns to his little spot in Georgia and begins to moan all over again. He once wrote to me 'I feel like a mangy ol' dog with sores on his ass stumbling along some hot asphalt in the noon-day sun. I have to keep stumbling on because if I sit down, my ass will burn'. He will never be able to opt out, yet he appears determined to keep trying. Occasionally I receive a long epistle bemoaning the futility of his efforts. I am always comforted by the predictability of his misery. It makes my own in politics so much more tolerable.

Two foreign academics whose friendships continue to mean a great deal to me are Theo Hanf and Heribert Adam. In both I sense a deep involvement in understanding the dynamics of social change in society and particularly in countries wrestling with the problems we face in South Africa. At the same time, their involvement is accompanied by a dispassionate and uncompromising assessment of the forces influencing the direction of change.

Our own domestic experts would agree that these two have an intimate knowledge of the working of those forces in South Africa.

I first met Hanf when I was still teaching at the University of Cape Town in 1971. He had started his research on the possibilities of peaceful change in South Africa. I was going to assist and hopefully write up a section on black and white student attitudes and involvement in change. A number of things happened to prevent this. I accepted the chair at Wits University in Johannesburg; there were some communication problems with Hanf's research institute in 1974. But I never lost touch with Hanf or the research he was busy with, and since going into politics I have managed to visit Freiburg more than half a dozen times.

Hanf has a country house in the Alsace near a little village called Metzeral, an hour-and-a-half away from Freiburg across the French border. There, together with others like Heribert Adam, Lawrence Schlemmer, Hennie Serfontein and colleagues from the Bergstraesser Institute, such as Heribert Weiland and Gerda Vierdag, we would talk into the early hours of the morning about what was likely to happen and what could be done in South Africa.

Heribert Adam is Professor of Sociology at Simon Fraser University in Vancouver. He wrote a book which has become a standard reference book on South Africa: *Modernizing Racial Domination*. I used it as a text-book long before I met him. Heribert enjoys running as much as I do and we have jogged together in the Black Forest, along the Rhine in Bad Godesberg and of course in Kirstenbosch in Cape Town. He has a gentle, almost self-effacing manner about him that can be deceptive because in academic debate I have always been impressed by his economy of formulation and his unerring ability to weed out the conceptual debris which clouds understanding. Both of them, Theo Hanf and Heribert Adam, unbeknown to them, have been my mentors, teaching me patience in promoting social change and intellectual discipline in understanding its complexity.

I suppose that is why Gérard Chaliand's book, *Revolution in the Third World: Myths and Prospects*, had such an immediate appeal for me. I discovered it quite by chance in the parliamentary library about 5 years ago, read it through almost in one sitting, right under the Speaker's nose, and equally coincidentally, met him a few weeks after I had read it. Like Hanf and Adam, who have not met him, he writes with candour and simplicity.

The Social Sciences unfortunately are burdened with unreadable doorstoppers, full of footnotes and jargon and over-generous homage to one of the founding fathers of one of the many ideological denominations, which obscure analysis of contemporary events. Chaliand's work was a succinct, comparative interpretation of the success, or failure, of revolutionary attempts in Africa, Asia and Latin America. He writes with analytical clarity and the benefit of experience. Chaliand certainly has a richness of experience which I envy. He was a young editor of a revolutionary journal in Algeria during the Revolution, knew the likes of Amilcar Cabral and Franz Fanon; had been in North Vietnam during the war and had recently visited a rebel encampment in Afghanistan. Having enjoyed it a few times before, I would walk more than a mile to enjoy a good meal and good wine in the pleasure of his company.

I have tried to explain to myself what it is, quite apart from their friendships, that attracts me to the thinking of people like Hanf, Adam and Chaliand. All of them in a sense are progenies of the intellectual ferment of Western Europe during the Sixties.

They studied under and were in touch with people such as Jean-Paul Sartre, Camus, Lévie Strauss, Habermas, Adorno and others. They were seduced by the romanticism of social change and how easy and necessary it was 'if only' X, Y and Z could be brought about, yet they never succumbed. Not one of them became intellectual junkies of the 'change industry', mouthing the shibboleths which guaranteed acceptance in academic circles where moral outbidding substituted for analysis.

Well, why do I like them? Because from them I learnt that your sense of moral outrage is no guarantee for the success of your political activism and certainly no precondition for effective change. There is no point in sacrificing what rationality you have simply because you are angry. Also, their disillusionment with grand theories of social change has not weakened their commitment to human dignity, freedom and justice – on the contrary, it has been strengthened. Furthermore, they are extremely conservative in their enthusiasm for the use of political power or violence by a few on behalf of many, whether the legitimizing ideology is from the right, left or even from 'above'. Finally, I suppose, it is the thinking of foreign academics such as these three, together with our own – such as André du Toit, Degenaar, Francis Wilson, Lawrence Schlemmer, Hermann Giliomee, David Welsh, Gavin Maasdorp, Jill Natrass, Charles van Onselen, Tony Mathews, John Dugard, Johan van Deventer and others – which holds the greatest promise for finding a way through our difficulties. They do not agree on many issues among themselves, but I find them remarkably free of the dogmatic confidence of the reigning academic establishments or schools on the left or right. For thirty-odd years we have had a school approach intellectually propping up apartheid; maybe a school approach from the left will be in at the kill in dismantling it – but I doubt its ability to solve the problems left in the aftermath, because the thinking is essentially the same. There is no greater danger to society than an academic who regards himself as a practical political expert, and whose confidence in his analytical framework outstrips his ability to come to terms with the socio-economic realities in which he lives. Give him power and he will prepare the groundwork for tyranny.

Of course Hanf and Adam's involvement in South Africa has a personal dimension to it as well. Hanf married Anne-Marie, a Lebanese girl, and became very interested in the political conflicts of that strife-torn society. His research led him to work on countries with similar problems such as the Sudan, Northern Ireland and South Africa.

In terms of South African law at the time, his marriage would be classified as mixed and therefore not recognized as legally valid. The same applied to Heribert Adam, who married Kogila, a South African Indian, a sociologist and a delightful human being. It defies credulity to listen to them recounting their experiences in South Africa as so-called 'mixed couples' whenever they have visited here.

But of course, the most dramatic instance of this absurdity in my own experience involves Breyten Breytenbach and Yolande; he an Afrikaner and she Vietnamese. I suppose I would never really have known Breyten if he had not been sent to prison for nine years in terms of the Terrorism Act. It is highly unlikely that Breyten would have become involved with revolutionary politics and the 'liberation' struggle in South Africa if the South African authorities had allowed him and Yolande to visit his own country and his parents, just like any normal young husband who wished to come and show off his beautiful new wife and to show her where he came from. But they refused her entry. Breyten went into voluntary exile for thirteen years and became heavily politicized about dramatic and radical change in South Africa. He returned with Yolande for the first time in 1972 and I met him very briefly when we shared a panel at Summer School at the University of Cape Town on *Die Sestigers*, a literary movement in Afrikaans predominant in the '60s. Apparently by then he was already deeply involved.

The next I heard of him was when he was arrested and charged under the Terrorism Act. The evidence in court painted a picture of political activism full of pathos and *naïveté*. Apparently he had hoped to establish an internal arm of a white resistance movement supplementary to the ANC, which was to be known as Okhela. Before he had even begun to recruit or establish any organizational infrastructure he was betrayed and arrested. This episode in his life is absorbingly described in his book *Confessions of an Albino Terrorist*. I was in the USA, in San Francisco, when I read that he had been sentenced to nine years in prison. Under the Terrorism Act there was no suspended sentence or parole possible. I was stunned at the severity of the punishment. It was the end of 1975.

At regular intervals after Breyten had gone to jail, I was approached by Afrikaans authors like André Brink and Jan Rabie to see if there was something that could be done to either effect Breyten's release or at least to improve the conditions of his release. I know that the same kind of petitioning was done in other quarters and perhaps with greater effect, so what I am about to recount is not an attempt to establish any claim to being solely responsible for Breyten's release.

Anyway that was not possible without the active co-operation of those in Government who had the final jurisdiction on matters of this kind, and in this respect nobody did more behind the scenes than the Minister involved, Kobie Coetsee.

For a number of reasons I had postponed asking permission to visit Breyten in jail: because I was not sure what I could say to him; was concerned that my visit would perhaps reduce his number of family visits; and that it would raise false hopes.

Late in 1981 I applied for such a visit despite these reservations and towards the end of the first quarter of 1982 had established a time when I could go and visit him in Pollsmoor Prison. I did not know what I was going to, or could, say to him, and it exercised my mind as I waited for the day to arrive. I was concerned that if my visit became known it would be dismissed as a publicity stunt, so very few people knew about it outside of the Prison Department and the relevant Minister.

In the meantime the No-Confidence Debate (1982) had come and gone and ended with quite an angry exchange between myself and Prime Minister P W Botha. He had referred to some remark I was supposed to have made at a cocktail party in Bonn, and I asked him whether he was having me followed. He said 'No', and I said, if he was he knew what he could do with his snoopers, and he said he would no longer talk to me, and so on. Typical parliamentary posturing from both of us.

For a week or two, things were icy between us; I made a point of greeting him formally every afternoon and he made a point of looking elsewhere. Then, quite out of the blue one Wednesday evening while I was listening to the MP for Rosettenville, who invariably fails to impress with the content of his speeches, but delivers them in delightful Afrikaans, the PM leant across and said to me 'Afrikaans is a beautiful language, is it not? I said, 'It certainly is', and for the time being peace had broken out between us. As I drove home I decided to seek an appointment with him and ask him to assist in the release of Breyten. The first thing next morning, I phoned the PM's office and asked for an appointment on a personal matter. By coincidence it was granted to me the very day after I was to see Breyten for the first time.

94

Pollsmoor Prison lies at the foot of the Kalk Bay mountains and on the edge of the Constantia Valley, one of the most beautiful suburbs of Cape Town. As often as I used to come over De Waal Drive on the way to Parliament and look towards Robben Island and think of Mandela and Sobukwe imprisoned there, I used to come over the mountains on Ou Kaapse Weg and think of Breyten sitting in Pollsmoor Prison.

I had never really talked to him before. We sat in an office in the presence of a prison officer and talked about inconsequential matters.

I told him that I was seeing the PM the next day and asked whether there was anything I could convey to him. He said he would appreciate a contact visit with Yolande – the kind of visit I was having with him at the moment (for the last six years he had talked to her on a telephone through a glass partition); also that he would appreciate it if some competent literary figure could be allowed to assess his prison work and if fellow authors and poets in addition to his family could visit him. As I left he gestured towards the prison officer present and said that he was grateful for his considerateness and that they had been in the same class at school together. He looked very fit, his beard was flecked with grey and it felt strange that I could not give him a lift into Cape Town when I said goodbye.

The Prime Minister was in a relaxed mood when I saw him the next day. I explained how his remark about Afrikaans the previous week had prompted me to seek an interview with him and then came straight to the point, saying that I wished him to use his personal influence in effecting the release of one of the masters of the Afrikaans language. His immediate reaction was sympathetic. The Breytenbach affair was a 'tragic situation', according to him; he came from a 'fine family' and his brothers, particularly the one in the Defence Force, had done 'commendable work' for South Africa.

However, the Prime Minister pointed out, Breyten had been found guilty in court and sentenced under a law of the country and this 'made it very difficult'. As tactfully as possible, I pointed out that he and his Government had made the law and therefore had the power to amend it. Again, he said he would consider the matter with 'great empathy'. I expressed my gratitude for his understanding and pointed out that this no doubt would take some time and that in the meantime there were other specific requests which I wished to convey to him arising out of my visit to Breyten the previous day, and which would significantly ease the conditions of imprisonment if granted. When I mentioned the 'contact visit' with Yolande and explained what was being asked, he appeared genuinely shocked that this had not happened before and promised to go into the matter.

And that is how I met Yolande and started my series of interviews and discussions with the then Minister of Prisons, Kobie Coetsee. Yolande is small, charming and gracious. My first impression of her was of her vulnerability, but this was soon dispelled. She is a person of great resolution and courage. Twice a year for seven years she would literally close shop, pack up and come to visit Breyten. Utterly tireless in her efforts to effect his release, she explored every possible avenue and opportunity. One simply had to read his poetry about her, and listen to her speak about him, to appreciate the strength of the bond between them and to realize that there was no law made by man that could make a dent in their love for each other.

I suppose it was this relationship more than Breyten's poetry (which I enjoy reading, but do not understand all that well) which motivated me to help Yolande while Breyten was in prison.

I did not speak to the Prime Minister about this matter again. He had obviously requested Kobie Coetsee to deal with it. I wish to put it on record that the Prime Minister never used or referred to this matter again in our public or personal interactions subsequently. It was a commitment that he honoured and which neither he nor I allowed to affect the quality of our exchanges afterwards. Kobie Coetsee as Minister of Prisons was sympathetic throughout our discussions, but extremely sensitive to the vested interests in the bureaucracies he had to deal with; particularly the Department of Prisons and the Security Police. Breyten himself makes it clear that personal vindictiveness in the Security Police undoubtedly prolonged the day of his release. Not knowing the inside story I thought Kobie Coetsee to be over-cautious in his dealings with the bureaucracies concerned. I will say this, however: he managed to get the relevant Acts amended which enabled a parole board to consider applications for so-called 'political prisoners'.

The press immediately started speculating about the possible release of Mandela and others who had been sentenced long before Breyten. After gauging the mood via my interviews with Kobie Coetsee, I appreciated how far off the mark they were. But, the machinery had been set in motion, it was now a question of setting it in motion as far as Breyten was concerned. It still took a long time.

In the meantime, 1982 had come and gone and I put in another application to visit Breyten in Prison. Kobie Coetsee said he thought this time it had to be a more formal visit. The 'Leader of the Opposition' being received by Pollsmoor and taken on a tour of inspection or something of that order. What followed was one of the most extraordinary experiences I have had.

I was picked up at about eleven o'clock one morning by General Otto, Director-General of Prisons: a jovial, overweight gentleman who died of a heart attack about eighteen months later. We left from Parliament in a chauffeur-driven Mercedes Benz. It took twenty minutes to Pollsmoor; General Otto chatting away in a friendly fashion. There we were met by Brigadier De Fortier, the Head of Pollsmoor and, I think, a Brigadier De Beer. While we were having a quick cup of tea we were told that we would inspect the various sections of the prison, after which we would have lunch. Till then not a word had been said about seeing Breyten.

We set off, General Otto and myself, following a Sergeant with a set of keys, and we in turn were followed by Brigadiers De Fortier and De Beer. The black women's section was the first to be inspected. At the main gate before the long corridor the Sergeant unlocked and shouted 'Attention!' into empty space. We heard some shuffling, and silence in response. The first cell had twelve female prisoners, each standing to attention next to a neatly made bed. There was a patient, sad look about them as they glanced over and past us.

General Otto walked up to the first one and said in a friendly voice, 'Well, sussie*, why are you here?'

She did not even turn to look at him as she said, 'Pass, my baas.'

The same response was forthcoming from the next three before the General stopped enquiring.

I know creative licence is often used to load moments with a significance far richer than experienced, but this was certainly not the case for me when I continued down the corridor towards the next point of inspection. I kept thinking, 'So this is where so many end up'.

* 'little sister'.

These prisoners were the wives of migrant labourers, who out of economic necessity gather their belongings and their children somewhere in the wastelands of rural poverty and move to search for and be with their husbands in the cities. For many, imprisonment is an inevitable ritual of urban migration. I thought of Lagos, Nairobi and of Crossroads, KTC, Winterveld, Kwamashu; of the worker who ordered his paralysed wife to drag herself across the floor to show me she was disabled; of the whole bureaucratic superstructure of routine indifference that rested on their suffering. Every year we make hundreds of thousands of technical criminals of simple folk who give vent to the most simple human needs: to look for work, shelter and to be together as families. We deem it appropriate to protect society from their 'crimes', lumping them together with thieves, murderers and common criminals. Somehow, the *sotto voce* 'Pass, my baas' of these women to General Otto was a moment or prismatic clarity to me, illuminating the monumental absurdity of the policy of separate development.

The next stop was a crèche for mothers who arrived pregnant in Pollsmoor. They stood around nursing or playing with the babies and again General Otto, with friendly resolution, approached one and asked her why she was here.

She looked him in the eye and with a slightly embarrassed smile said, 'Soliciting in the Docks!'

'Naughty, naughty', said the General and we all laughed conspiratorially with a 'sailors-will-be-sailors' kind of wisdom.

We then went through the kitchen into the white male section. I noticed all the prisoners standing on pieces of cloth about half a square metre in size. These were known as 'taxis'; prisoners shuffled around on them before inspection so as not to dirty the floor and of course, to keep it nice and shiny bright. One fellow in his mid-thirties, with two front teeth missing and a brush cut, stood rigidly to attention as the General asked him why he was here.

'Sodomy,' he said, and we moved on without further comment.

About forty-five minutes before lunch, the General drew me aside and said he believed I would like to see Breyten. We walked across some court-yard into what looked like an administrative section. He opened an office door and there stood Breyten. The General excused himself and we were completely alone; apparently a rare exception. I

98

remember encouraging him not to lose hope and telling him that things were moving and that when last I saw Yolande she was in good spirits. I sensed a special pressure in his greeting when we shook hands in parting. I joined the General and the two Brigadiers for lunch and thanked them for their considerateness. We sat down to a meal at a long rectangular table; each one of us on a side with a single bottle of Nederburg Paarl Riesling, a forlorn little Eiffel Tower, right in the middle on a silver tray. The General asked Brigadier De Fortier to say grace so that we could proceed with a clear conscience.

In the meantime, Mandela and some others had been moved from Robben Island to Pollsmoor Prison. Driving out of Pollsmoor after lunch I small-talked the General about this and he turned around and pointed to a section with a tower and said, 'Yes, he is there'.

'Why was he moved?' I asked.

'He was getting too bossy and influential on the Island,' said the General.

'Oh', I said, 'and who is the leader on the island now?'

'Man, what's-his-name, that coolie, Kathrada,' said the General.

He dropped me off at Parliament and I thanked him again for his courtesy and his time. The bells had already gone and the afternoon's business was proceeding. Someone was droning away on some bill or the other. Some were bowing in and out to the Speaker and others were quietly munching toffees or sucking peppermints after lunch. It was an unexceptional afternoon in Parliament.

Christmas was again approaching and it seemed that Breyten was going to spend another one in prison. Yolande was in the country again and when we talked she said that she was quite desperate and did not know what to expect. I shared her desperation, but said to her I thought another visit to the Minister, Kobie Coetsee, could possibly shed some new light.

I flew to Pretoria and talked to Kobie in his offices in the Sanlam building. He seemed nervous and excited, would not say much and kept exhorting me not to lose hope. I asked him whether Yolande should extend her ticket or keep it as booked.

He saw the trap, smiled and said, 'Tell her to be patient'.

I told her I thought something was definitely in the air.

Three days before her ticket was due to expire, in the second week of December, I again phoned Kobie and explained Yolande's predicament to him. He told me to wait twenty-four hours. He phoned the next day, asking me where Yolande would be at lunch-time. I gave him Revel and Suzanne Fox's address in Newlands and he said he thought it was time us politicians withdrew from the scene and that I must promise him not to see Breyten or exploit the situation politically in any way. (In waiting more than two years, I think I have kept my promise.) I saw Yolande briefly at the Fox's home and told her I thought Breyten's release was imminent. We said good-bye, but I do not think she heard a word I was saying. The next morning Suzanne Fox brought me a letter Breyten had written in the early hours of the morning in which he said we must definitely crack a bottle together in Paris at the very first opportunity. I knew then that he had really been released.

He hurriedly travelled to Grahamstown (with a Professor in Afrikaans literature who had been allowed to appraise his work in prison) to see his ailing father before he and Yolande flew out of the country to Paris.

The year 1983 was referendum year. Breyten and I did not correspond. In the meantime, Rabkin, Cronin and Kidson had been released in the same way as Breyten. In early December I attended, together with other members of my party, a conference at Gummersbach near Bonn, arranged by the Friedrich Naumann Foundation, and I phoned Breyten beforehand saying I could spend two days in Paris for a reunion. It was all arranged.

But before Paris I went to London to see Ian Jones. We had been students at Stellenbosch and played first team rugby together. He became a bit of a legend at Stellenbosch as an outsider, rebel and incorrigible subverter of the University establishment. Despite, or perhaps because of these adverse recommendations, he managed to get a Rhodes Scholarship to Oxford, where he achieved Blues for Boxing and Rugby, performed well academically, and was *persona non grata* in most of the pubs in Oxford. We saw each other again after Stellenbosch when I visited Oxford on an Abe Bailey Travel Bursary in 1964, and in the Blue Room, Jones and I discovered that the two of us were born on the same date.

This bit of profound historical coincidence precipitated one of the most prolonged bouts of irrelevant celebration I can remember. I was staying in one of the University residences and the gates had long since been locked when Jones and I managed to navigate ourselves to one of the side walls of the residence. He assisted me in scaling it, all the while explaining where, more or less, my room was likely to be. It was December and snowing. My coat got hooked on something and I hung on the wall in mid-air. Jones climbed over to unhook me and fell into the rose garden. My laughter tore my coat off the hook and I fell into the rose garden as well. We ended up in the Warden's residence staging a mock bullfight with his academic caps and gowns. The lights went on, Jones ran off in one direction and I in another. We did not see each other for ten years after that, until I visited London again as the MP for Rondebosch. Since then we get together as often as possible just to enjoy each other's company. As I said before, he is a great companion.

One of our obligatory rituals is to go to Animos (a Greek Cypriot restaurant) in Charlotte Street to eat kleftikon and drink retsina. Oblivion and therapy are also offered at no extra charge. Many times, Jones and I would dance and sing and curse the Devil into the early hours.

And so it was before I went to see Breyten and Yolande for the reunion in Paris. This time I needed it too. I had just been through a referendum, which said yes to a disastrous constitution; Pitman had died four weeks before and I was ragged. Earlier in the year my divorce had been finalized after eighteen years of marriage. It is pointless to recriminate or scratch about for the whys and hows of my divorce. Politics undoubtedly placed an enormous load on our relationship and she tried to be as supportive as possible in what must have been as strange a world to her as it was to me. Obviously we had hurt and misunderstood each other. In the end new mistakes compounded old ones in a cycle of increasing alienation that became too painful to endure. Now I am grateful that enough compassion remains to combat bitterness and leave the love for our children uncontaminated.

Although it had been a rough year, there were good signs too. I had met someone and fallen in love in the good old-fashioned way. Now, in retrospect, it was one of the best things that ever happened to me. We are married and every day is fresh and new. Nothing has assaulted my cynicism as successfully as our relationship and through Jane I have appreciated Breyten and Yolande even more. That was the other good thing that night in Animos and, of course, the prospect of seeing them again.

Jones was going to Paris as well. He and some Welsh friends had decided to watch the rugby match between Wales and France in Paris, so I went along for the ride. France won; the Welshmen were devastated and I got pick-pocketed of R200 on the Metro from the Parc de Prince after the game. Breyten had booked me into a small hotel on the Left Bank, Hotel Alsace Lorraine in Rue de Canettes. Jones and I were stumbling down the street with our baggage toward the Hotel when suddenly Breyten stood there. I had not seen him since that extraordinary day in Pollsmoor Prison. We embraced and laughed and talked till one o'clock that morning. We agreed to meet again in a few hours' time. Yolande and Breyten left. Jones and I were so elated that we kept on talking and walking the streets. Three o'clock found us having bouillabaisse in a restaurant two streets from our Hotel.

We parted early that morning and Breyten picked me up with Yolande and a friend and we went to an exhibition of Buddhist murals from the Gobi Desert in a huge hot-house kind of structure in a park somewhere near the Notre Dame.

I was tired, but very pleased with myself. I remember experiencing a sentimental pride listening to Breyten explain the intricacies of Buddhist paintings to me as we walked from one room to the next and kept on thinking, 'he is the best kind of Afrikaner we have produced'. I tend to think in hyperbole when I am fatigued. But now, refreshed and reflective, I still think so.

He took me to Charles de Gaulle airport in a taxi talking unsolicitedly about Pollsmoor Prison all the way. I was impressed by his lack of bitterness and self-pity. From what he said it was a vastly different place to the one I had experienced, and he told me he was going to write it all up. Having read *Confessions of an Albino Terrorist* I know now what he tried to convey then.

As I flew to Frankfurt en route to Jan Smuts, Johannesburg, I thought of the year ahead, 1984, and the impending implementation of the new Constitution. If Breyten and Yolande, Theo and Anne-Marie Hanf and Heribert and Kogila Adam were to live in South Africa once that constitution became reality, the husbands would have to vote for representation in the white chamber, and the wives in either the Coloured or Indian chambers; they would have to live in separate Group Areas unless special dispensation could be arranged; and their children would have to go to private schools, because no Government school would be able to accommodate them.

It was an essential arrangement of the new Constitution that the laws which prescribed this should remain part of it. Sixty percent of the whites had voted yes for the implementation of this constitution, because as some of them said: 'At least it was a step in the right direction'.

'CHEE-RIST', I could hear Pitman shout, 'we're all stark raving crazy!'

The demise of the last white Parliament

And so the last session of the all-white Parliament began in January 1984. I had been in politics for ten years. What had changed? Change is an important word for politicians. We use it to beguile, predict and bewilder. Above all, we always claim credit for whatever benefit it brings and charge its drawbacks to the account of our opponents.

If nothing else had changed, it was certainly not true as far as I was concerned. In ten years I had scaled down the scope of my predictions; moderated some key assumptions of my understanding of our society and become humbled, sometimes even humiliated by experience, but the fire still raged in my belly for things I wanted to do and see happen and against things I could not accept. Concerning the political situation in my country I remain unresolved about more things than not.

For ten years I had come to Parliament – this corporate entity in the 'change industry' of South Africa; the white man's last remaining, deeply flawed tribute to democracy on the continent – to listen and to speak.

There are many barometers of change in our society: the interaction between unrest and repression; economic growth and unemployment; management-labour disputes; population increase and shifts; constitutional and unconstitutional politics; parliamentary and extra-parliamentary action. But Parliament, for the time being, remains the most reliable barometer of change in Government rhetoric and policy. From it, one can gauge how Government perceives threat and opportunity and how it wishes to cope with either.

And there, too, changes have taken place. In the first place it is quite clear that those who govern have lost the ideological solidarity which first united them as a party. Bluntly, they no longer believe apartheid or separate development is going to pull us through. This loss of dogmatic confidence is reflected in the change of rhetoric as well. Today the Government talks about negotiation and consultation rather than confrontation or take-it-or-leave-it politics. Consensus and compromise are praised instead of unilateral demands on any side. At the same time, the degree of repressive tolerance has increased as this new rhetoric has flourished. Coercion and repression of extra-parliamentary opposition has become far more subtle and sophisticated. It would be very foolish to interpret this loss of ideological cohesion and the new 'reasonable rhetoric' as symptoms of a loss of will to dominate.

Parliament has also been increasingly excluded from the military actions of Government. Clandestine operations increased as the 'total onslaught' ideology developed, and those in opposition invariably found themselves confronted with *post facto* accounts of expeditions whose immediate necessity was impossible to assess because of the secrecy which surrounded them. Now it is clear that neighbouring countries have been 'thumped and talked' into a regional dependence on and submission to South Africa. This, of course, has the effect of making it more difficult to find credible scapegoats to fill the script in the 'total onslaught' drama. Inevitably, as the external onslaught subsides, the 'internal onslaught' will come under sharper focus – the enemy without will become the enemy within. I fear that the Government has in any case managed to militarize the white population to such an extent that it won't matter much to the ordinary person who the 'enemy' is, as long as he is ready to fight him. Therein, I believe, lies one of the greatest obstacles to evolutionary and negotiated change.

Of course, the most significant change as far as Parliament is concerned, was the change of Parliament itself by means of a new constitution for the Republic of South Africa.

This hallowed sanctuary of white sovereignty and domination was going to change its composition to allow Coloureds and Asians to become part of it and observe how power is exercised, controlled and above all, guarded. Those who promoted it hailed this as a 'new beginning', a 'step in the right direction', towards a destination which even now is shrouded in the mists of obscurity. P W Botha even claimed it was a form of 'healthy power-sharing' as opposed to 'unhealthy power-sharing' (which I and my party and some others apparently stood for).

Ever since its inception the concept of power-sharing epitomized political blasphemy to the Nationalist Party (come to think of it, at the outset they were not into sharing anything, whether it be land, money or toilets.) That is why when P W Botha referred to the new constitutional proposals in this fashion, it was sufficient reason for a group of Nationalists in Parliament under the leadership of Dr Andries Treurnicht to break away. They seized on this opportunity to settle a host of other political and personal differences by splitting, and immediately began to ascribe profound ideological import to their breakaway.

However, in the eyes of many well-intentioned reformers, the mere fact of the split was sufficient to sanction the new Constitution, irrespective of its contents or merits. The argument was – if Botha had the 'courage' to split his party, then the proposals simply had to be good. A powerful and compelling *non-sequitur*. As Murphy would say: 'Nothing is as inevitable as a mistake whose time has arrived'.

The fact is that the new Constitution has very little to do with power-sharing. It merely changes the status of the Coloured and Asian minorities from being repressively dominated to being co-optively dominated. Because they themselves assist in its administration from the central institution of power, namely Parliament, the quality of their domination by the rulers is softened. The most visible change for these minorities as a result of this co-option will lie in the nature of political patronage at their disposal.

The Nationalist Government has tried various co-optive strategies with blacks, Coloureds and Asians over the years. (In fact, the homelands policy, even to its logical conclusion, is nothing but a policy of co-optive domination.) However, the rule had always been to co-opt other groups into separate/segregated/apart political structures *away* from the centre of power, and then to dominate from a distance by means of budgetary or coercive measures.

This new Constitution co-opted people who were not white *into* the centre of political power, although still in segregated structures. It was a shift from *exclude*-divide-and-rule to *include*-divide-and-rule. This inclusion, rather than any clearly definable power-sharing, 'healthy' or otherwise, was what Treurnicht and company found so objectionable. And understandably so, because co-optive domination into the power centre was a shift away from NP orthodoxy.

In this shift the dynamics of the new political situation will have to be explored. But these dynamics will have very little to do with the contents and merits of the new constitution itself.

As a constitution it is a thoroughly bad one. Bad in the manner in which it evolved, bad in its design and, I fear, even clumsier in its execution. How did this sorry mess come about? There are a few footpaths which all lead to the same clearing in our domestic political jungle.

The first has to do with the actions (or lack thereof) of the first President's Council. As I have said before, the creation of this Council was P W Botha's response to having inherited a set of constitutional proposals from the 1977 Vorster General Election.

Apparently the white electorate gave them massive endorsement but no-one else wanted them, including the so-called Coloureds and Indians who were supposed to be the major beneficiaries. First, a parliamentary Select Committee was created to investigate the introduction of a new constitution. Its majority report recommended the creation of an advisory President's Council. The composition of the Council excluded blacks and those who served on it were in effect nominated by the Prime Minister. It was supposed to be stocked with experts from various fields, but as it turned out, with a few exceptions, the President's Council became the grazing ground for political has-beens rewarded for loyal service, or a hitching post for others waiting for vacancies to occur elsewhere.

However, it did have the task ostensibly to advise the Government on further constitutional development. On the President's Council two sub-committees took this duty seriously: the Constitutional Sub-Committee with Dr Dennis Worrall as Chairman and the Economic Sub-Committee with Dr Schalk van der Merwe as Chairman.

Immediately there appeared to be two competing approaches to constitutional change: one from local to central Government, from the 'bottom up', as it were, the other from central to local Government, from the 'top down'.

The former was a piecemeal, building block approach under Schalk van der Merwe; the other was a holistic framework approach under Dennis Worrall. It soon became apparent that the Sub-Committee under Van der Merwe was progressing at a faster pace than the one under Worrall and would have its report completed first. This was not on as far as Dennis Worrall was concerned, and I suspect that between him and Professor de Crespigny they scrambled together a report which they rushed through their Sub-Committee and tabled as the Constitutional Sub-Committee's recommendations. The report was an embarrassment and an insult to anyone's intelligence. Apart from using some pseudo-consociational claptrap to justify black exclusion from the same constitution as whites, Coloureds and Asians, it recommended virtually *carte blanche* powers to an executive President to create his own constitution for Coloureds, Asians and whites. Van der Merwe's Sub-Committee produced a report which at least deserved some serious attention, but left crucial areas vacant because it became trapped in its own racial logic. For the time being however, this report was shifted into the background.

But what to do about the Worrall Report? Enter Minister Chris Heunis. He saw how untenable the President's Council Report was. (I do not know what happened behind the scenes; rumours had it that Heunis and Worrall became increasingly alienated from one another.)

In any case, it is of no consequence. The Worrall report was shelved and he became Ambassador to Australia. Heunis and his assistants dusted off the old 1977 proposals and started streamlining them. It is well to remember that the 1977 proposals had already been cleared and approved by the Nationalist Party parliamentary caucus, so that obstacle had been taken care of. Therefore, without substantially altering the contents of the 1977 proposals, the illusion could be created that an entirely new set of proposals had been produced. But instead of three Parliaments segregated on racial lines there would be one Parliament with three Chambers, segregated along racial lines, and so on. After this constitutional tinkering, the 'new' set of proposals was paraded before all the Nationalist Party Provincial as well as Federal Congresses for approval. They were endorsed according to the tried and tested formula of confronting party formations with preprocessed decisions, the import of which they had insufficient time to study and on which they were hence incompetent to express meaningful opinions. Consequently unanimous endorsements with thunderous acclaim were the order of the day.

But it would appear that we had come full circle. Were we not back to 1977 where the Nationalist Party had produced a set of constitutional proposals that were supposedly heavily endorsed by the white electorate in a general election, but which nobody else wanted?

On the surface of it, yes. However, there were two new intervening variables on the scene this time: the personality and position of Chris Heunis, and the internal developments and changes within the (Coloured) Labour Party. Heunis came into prominence under P W Botha's premiership. As I said before he is an intelligent, forceful, if somewhat overbearing personality. It is to his credit that he saw immediately that what was missing in the 1977 attempt was political marketing. A take-it-or-leave-it attitude towards the Coloureds and Asians was simply not going to work. Heunis, more than anyone else in the Nationalist Party ranks, popularized the rhetoric of reform and negotiation. He was the past master at talking consensus without making binding concessions. This is exactly what he did with the Labour Party. He wooed, cajoled and pleaded with them. He hinted, suggested and implied, but not once was a definite public promise extracted or a definite shift in Nationalist Party policy offered. The success of Heunis's lobbying became obvious when, on 4 January 1983, the Coloured Labour Party held its annual Congress in Zululand and decided to participate in the new constitution – whatever it was going to be. (Up till then, it had not even been presented to Parliament as a Bill.)

It is not always easy to identify a clearcut precipitating factor that sets off a train of historical events. That is why there is scope for more than one historian to offer his interpretation of history.

But I have little doubt that Hendrickse's* decision precipitated the implementation of the new constitution. Till then the Government was uncertain if it should press ahead with its proposals. These were laughed out of court by every respectable academic and newspaper editor, and even within the Nationalist Party response to them was lukewarm to say the least. However, a great deal of political energy had been invested in them, and political reputations were at stake. Not least of which were those of Prime Minister P W Botha and his trusted lieutenant Chris Heunis. The Eshowe decision blessed all their efforts and kicked off the constitutional change we now have to live with.

It was an extraordinary decision by all accounts. It was taken without knowing what the final constitutional package was going to be,

* Leader of the Labour Party and now a Cabinet Minister.

nor with any ostensible concessions having been bargained as part of that package. And then Chief Gatsha Buthelezi*, head of the black Alliance of which the Labour Party was a member (and who had on numerous occasions voiced his opposition to, and rejection of the proposals) had been invited to be guest of honour, only to hear for the first time that the Labour Party was going to participate. It made no sense, except if one concluded that within the inner circles of the Labour Party it had been decided that they were going in, come what may. If anything was a tribute to Chris Heunis's persuasive powers, it was the subsequent decision of the Labour Party Executive on 4 January 1983.

This set the stage for the 1983 Session of Parliament and for the passage of the South African Constitution Amendment Bill. Early on in the session the Prime Minister announced that a referendum would be held for whites to determine the acceptability of the new Constitution. When the Bill was first tabled it soon became clear that it was a hotch-potch of contradictory and divergent constitutional principles. One thing was apparent though: although Coloureds and Asians had been brought on board, nothing was going to affect the dominant position of the white minority, nor were the racist laws underpinning the system of apartheid going to be scrapped or fundamentally amended. The Constitution made it quite clear that it was entirely possible to phase out the last white Parliament without relinquishing white domination.

On the contrary, clients other than whites could be co-opted to service that domination. The acid test would be whether or not such clients were going to play ball in terms of the fundamental assumptions of white domination; whether or not they had their own hidden agendas. So far the agendas remain extremely well concealed, but in the likelihood of interest groups using the same instrument to pursue alternative goals, lies the dynamics of co-optive politics.

It was a long Bill and a complicated Constitution. In steering it through Parliament, Heunis was at his arrogant, eloquent and contemptuous best.

Speaking twice as long as anybody else, he regularly complained

---

* Also President of Inkatha, a Zulu based movement which has almost a million signed up members.

that the other side was wasting time. Eventually the Government moved the 'guillotine motion' which meant that after Clause 34 of a 104 Clause Bill no more debate was allowed in Committee stage. The public certainly was not going to get too much detail about the possible workings of the new Constitution. In any case, the impression seemed to be that now that the Nationalist Party Congresses and the Labour Party had blessed whatever was going to be the final package by their participation in it, it was pointless to waste too much parliamentary debate on it.

The other outstanding issue was what the question was going to be for the white referendum. I thought there was a slender hope if the Government undertook a genuine test of white electoral attitudes, that the constitution could be placed in better perspective. With this in mind, I suggested to the Prime Minister that three questions rather than a simple Yes/No be asked.

The three I suggested were: '(a) Do you believe that only whites should participate in Parliament?; (b) Do you believe that only whites, Coloureds and Asians should participate in Parliament?; (c) Do you believe that whites, Coloureds, Asians and blacks should participate in Parliament without one group dominating the others?'

I argued that the response to these questions would clearly identify the scope for reform or the strength of reaction to it, and at the same time would leave the Prime Minister with enough flexibility to decide whether he should proceed with the implementation of the Constitution or not.

I also pointed out that the same questions could be put to Coloureds, Asians and blacks, to get the feeling from these communities. The Prime Minister thanked me for the trouble I had gone to, politely took my questions, and a few weeks later announced a simple Yes/No question in Parliament. I immediately pointed out that the question was highly ambiguous and that replies to it would not enable anyone to infer how many said yes to keep blacks out or to bring them in, nor how many who said no did so because Coloureds and Asians were included, or because blacks were excluded. The Prime Minister smiled and licked his lips in that familiar way of his. I could see he knew I was in for a beating. It was the kind of political contest he relished.

But it was not only the ineptitude of the Constitutional Committee of the President's Council, with the role of Chris Heunis and the vacillation of the Labour Party which heralded the demise of the last white Parliament. Combined with all this, the Nationalist Party Information Department had discovered the power of political marketing on a grand scale. The 1983 referendum if nothing else, was a superb marketing success for the Government. Ironically, they employed some individuals who had served the Progressive Federal Party interests with great distinction in the 1981 General Election – individuals who assured us then that there was no way they could help us if they did not 'believe' in the product they were selling.

This obviously applied again for the Nationalist Party in 1983. No expense or effort was spared. In fact, the Government spent more on full-page advertisements in the Sunday press on one day than the PFP had to spend on the whole referendum campaign; and even then they maintained the illusion that we are a rich man's party tied to the apron strings of corporate South Africa. In fact, nothing could be further from the truth. The business community had bought the Yes vote – if not the constitution – hook, line and sinker. It was pathetic to listen to them discussing the presumed benefits for South Africa and 'the world' of a constitution about which most of them did not have even the faintest idea. When at a private dinner party I enquired of one extremely influential businessman whether he had actually read the constitution, he became puce with irritation and said to me: 'I haven't read it, and have no intention of reading it. It's your problem to explain to me why I should not support it'. With that logic pervading the pub talk in the Rand Club, I and my party did not stand a chance. Already the information was filtering back to me that I was 'too negative', 'too radical', had been influenced by the 'leftist clique in my own caucus' – of course it was a lot of balls.

There were significant exceptions in the business community as well. Funnily enough, almost without exception objections came from those who had actually read and understood the new constitution, people like Tony Bloom, Gordon Waddell, Clive Menell and H F Oppenheimer were quite clear in their rejection of it.

I might as well dispel a popular myth now that I have mentioned H F Oppenheimer. In some quarters it is still held that when he cracks the whip I jump; that he virtually decides my party's strategy as well as that of the English press. This is political fiction at its worst. In fact, we see each other perhaps once or twice a year when we can have an in-depth discussion about current events. He has never tried to influence my decisions, but I have found him one of the most cultured human beings I have met, full of wisdom and sound political instinct. Despite his wealth and international interests, I know him to be very seriously interested in this country and its future, and this to me is enough reason to treat his counsel with respect.

H F Oppenheimer hosted a lunch for me to which most of the top English-speaking businessmen came. Almost without exception they agreed with my reasons for rejecting the new constitution, but at the same time, it was clear to me that most of them were going to support the Yes vote. This was the most extraordinary thing about this referendum: the Yes vote had absolutely nothing to do with the merits of the constitution. Through skilful marketing, the Government was selling 'reform', 'steps in the right direction', 'goodness', 'happiness', 'positiveness', every emotion and value it could dredge up. The 1983 referendum showed me that intelligent, successful people can collectively abandon reason and common sense.

It was also the first time that the Government had manipulated television and the radio bluntly and shamelessly as part of their marketing campaign. In fact, a senior Nationalist MP told me how a group of them would get together every day and plan what was going to be shown from all parties that evening. I believe this because at one meeting I made a public request to the South African Broadcasting Corporation to show a specific extract of a speech of mine the following evening. They did not. The Government even brought back our ambassadors from the United Kingdom, United States of America and West Germany and paraded them on the screen, where they solemnly declared how 'the world' was waiting with bated breath for a Yes vote, and the blessings that would flow to South Africa if this were successful. Absolutely nauseating stuff. I have no objection to political marketing. But what I could not understand was the lack of awareness of the Government and sections of the media that what was at issue was not simply an electoral victory of a particular party, the consequences of which could be absorbed by subsequent developments, but in fact a new constitution for the country, which would prescribe the rules of the political game. In terms of it we were going to have to resolve our conflicts and attempt further evolutionary and constitutional change. This fact alone should have made it imperative not only to scrutinize the potential of that constitution, but to inform the public as thoroughly as possible about ramifications.

Of course, there is one very important assumption underlying this lament of mine. That is that whatever its specific content, 'reform' of some kind or other was the motivating factor behind the introduction of the constitution. I could not understand how the same laws that were the critical issues of reform – the Population Registration Act and the Group Areas Act – could be built into the very structure of the constitution and that the constitution still had to be the instrument to reform those laws. In addition it made absolutely no sense, if you accepted that the legitimacy of reform also depended on the acceptance of the constitution by a significant number of blacks, deliberately to exclude them from the working of the constitution itself. It was Henry Kissinger who made clear to me, unintentionally perhaps, that reform itself was not the main consideration behind the constitution, if indeed it were a reason at all. On his visit to South Africa in 1983 we had breakfast together in the State House in Pretoria. He came straight to the point saying that we could either spend time exchanging pleasantries or he would play devil's advocate by defending the new constitution (which he said he had not read), whilst I explained my objections to it. He was extraordinarily skilful. What came out of his defence was not the need for reform, but how a dominant minority intent on maintaining control could manipulate patronage by co-opting clients to assist it.

Unbeknown to Kissinger, the result of that breakfast was, for me, the clarification of the idea of co-optive domination. But this was certainly not what was being 'sold' to the white electorate. If only it were, I believed, we would not be heading for disillusionment. The whites were being fed on a heavy diet of 'reform' and 'steps in the right direction'. There was *naïveté* to the belief that because Coloureds and Asians were being co-opted into the political centre, some 'movement', 'change', 'reform' was inevitable. I feared then, and I still do, that nothing was going to give 'reform' as bad a name as a constitution that was brought into being by its promise, but proved incapable of bringing it about.

Another significant development brought about by the referendum concerned the English press. It has been considered axiomatic ever since 1948 (when the present Government came into power) that the

English press opposed it and, with varying degrees of enthusiasm, supported the official opposition or parties considered left of it. I have always thought it a gross over-simplification to treat the English press as a collective entity. The English press was far less tied to party political dogma than the Afrikaans press. In fact, it is difficult after ten years in politics to tell anyone what the political solution for South Africa's problems is that enjoys the unqualified support of the majority of editors of English newspapers and magazines.

In this sense, the English press is symptomatic of the ideological diversity of opposition to the Government, rather than representing a clearly defined alternative. Nevertheless, the English press, broadly speaking, used to take an opposition line. Not this time however. There were crows of delight from the Nationalist press when significant defections to the Yes vote became apparent in the form of the *Sunday Times* and the *Financial Mail*. The editors of both agreed that the new constitution was an abortion and 'fatally flawed', but nevertheless urged their readers to vote Yes because it was 'at least a step in the right direction'. This was a 'can't lose' as opposed to a 'can't win' situation. If the constitution turned out to be an abortion, they at least had tried to make the best of it, and if it did not turn out to be a complete abortion, they could claim that this was so because they had tried to make the best of it. Obviously, editors are and should be entirely free to write whatever they wish, and there is not one that can claim that I tried to influence him to write what I would like to see. (Not that I have any such influence in any case.) But I simply cannot follow the reasoning that utterly condemned something which they then encouraged others to support.

One incident provided a slightly more chilling and disconcerting side to this paradox. A very influential English newspaper editor was kind enough to visit me in my office to listen to my objections to the new constitution before he informed me that he had decided to support it in any case.

Again my reasons were accepted as valid and self-evident, but the editor then went on to say that the new constitution was the most that could be expected from this Government and then these words: 'In any case, democracy simply does not work in Africa.' Now, for me, two things are important about this kind of journalistic nihilism. The assumption is that not only is democracy 'not for South Africa', but

115

also that it is not even worth trying to promote it. At best what we must settle for is some benign form of racial domination: 'Thank God, we whites are doing the dominating so at least it is vastly more sophisticated and intelligent than what is going on in the rest of Africa'. This is the ideology of domination in its most appealing, rational and pragmatic form. The second conclusion I draw from the statement is that, whilst to such people 'democracy is not for South Africa', it is still expedient and even fashionable to them to use democratic values in promoting the new constitution. It is 'broadening the base of democratic participation', at least 'they (blacks) are brought into the decision-making process'. Ironically, this is exactly the logic used by other African heads of state to justify one-party states and life Presidencies. Every time I recall that editor's words I can hear the youngsters in the bush and in our black townships saying 'Amen' to the ideology of liberation and revolution. After all, if the name of the game is domination, why settle for white if you are black?

What I found totally lacking on the part of those high-powered highly intelligent people who supported the Yes vote whilst condemning the constitution, was an appreciation of the interaction between white initiative and black response when it came to constitutional change. There was a very simple test for establishing this interaction throughout the white referendum campaign: at no stage would even half of the Coloureds, Asians and certainly blacks come out in full support of this constitution in a truly nationwide referendum. To me it seems elementary that if you embark on the risky business of changing the constitution of a country, those who do it and support it should have reasonable grounds for believing that the new constitution will have more legitimacy and support than the old one. In the South African context, such legitimacy and support certainly did not depend on white response to the constitution, but on acceptance of it by those who had been excluded from the existing one. Not even the Coloured Labour Party claimed to be representative of the excluded majority.

So what was the secret, what was the alchemy which would somehow make the new constitution work despite its obvious flaws? I could never quite put my finger on it when reading the enthusiastic supporters of the Yes vote who condemned the constitution. Phrases such as 'it depends on goodwill on all sides for it to work', 'the confusion created by the obvious shortcomings will unleash new forces for change', 'the Nats can never go back after this', seemed to bring comfort to them, but never was there any coherent analysis to back this up or even the slightest empirical evidence to support it. It was thumbsucking and wishful thinking on an impressive scale. But it was extremely successful.

We, that is, the PFP, had a very simple message which we put forward in the campaign. The new constitution could not be supported because:

> It was one party's solution imposed on the rest of the country; it excluded blacks from its workings and therefore would polarize black/white and promote conflict and dissatisfaction; it entrenched racial laws which lay at the heart of apartheid as we and the rest of the world came to know it; and it gave too much power to the new executive President.

This approach was considered 'negative', 'short-sighted' and 'out of touch' with contemporary developments in the country.

Instead, we were told that a successful Yes vote would 'usher in a new era of consensus politics', 'promote domestic racial peace' and understanding, move us away from 'confrontationist politics'; increase 'international understanding' and 'decrease pressure'. Some even went so far as to say that 'foreign capital' would flow into the country and that Moscow was waiting in gleeful anticipation for a No vote to succeed. A year after the outcome of the referendum, I had no reason whatsoever to reconsider any of the objections which we voiced against the constitution and I could say it without any satisfaction. We have wasted precious time and I am afraid we are going to continue to do so for some time to come. All the scenes of this farce have not been played out yet.

The referendum ended on a high note for P W Botha and the Government. Almost 66% of the white electorate voted yes. As the *Sunday Times* put it: it was 'go, go, go' for the Constitution. The *Financial Mail* patronizingly told me and my party that hopefully we had learnt a lesson, would stop being silly and get on with the job or something to that effect. Others predicted the imminent demise of the PFP, and that 'our job' would be taken over by the Coloureds and

Asians and that in the 'new style of politics' there was not really any scope for a party such as ours. (Of course all this could turn out to be true, but certainly not for the reasons that were being put forward.)

The Prime Minister was right: we had taken a beating; in fact even greater than I had anticipated. There is no question, that quite apart from the successful marketing campaign of the Government, the line that I took as Leader of the party must have played a role as well. I was quite happy to resign if this was felt necessary, because as I told the National Congress of the PFP two weeks after the referendum, if confronted with the same circumstances, I would do the same again. It must have been difficult for some of my caucus members to stick to the line in the face of such strong establishment support for a Yes vote, but almost without exception they did so loyally. You certainly learn who to take along on a desert walk on such occasions. At the same Party Congress I also committed the party to participating in the new constitution, should it become reality. (My own feeling was that we should not commit ourselves until at least a majority of Coloureds and Asians voted yes in a similar referendum. I was amused at the thought of how surprised those who claimed that I was the victim of a 'leftist liberal clique' in the party would be if they knew who eventually exhorted me not to follow this line of brinkmanship.) The decision to participate in the new Constitution despite our vigorous objection to it was interpreted as an about face by some, and even a betrayal of principles by others. It is neither. There is a clear difference between endorsing a constitution and participating in it.

If we hoped to influence constitutional change we had to explore the possibilities of such a process by participating in the constitution even though it was totally inadequate to meet the political needs of those subjected to it. The same had been true of our participation in the previous one and there was no reason why it should not be true for this one as well. There was a major mistake I did make, however. I believe I should have been far more insistent on referenda for Coloureds, Asians and blacks (after all they were going to be affected much more by their exclusion from it, as Coloureds and Asians were presumably going to be by their inclusion, than we were). I have no doubt that if they had been held, the results would have made it impossible for the Government to continue with its implementation of the new constitution.

The 1984 session was a lame duck session of Parliament in the sense of waiting for the new constitution to become reality. Three things still had to take place before this, however: new Standing Rules and Orders had to be formulated for the new tri-cameral system; Coloured and Indian elections had to be held (by then it had become clear that no referenda for them similar to that for whites were going to be held.) In fact, again the Labour Party did not demand this, but were eager for elections because a referendum 'would simply confuse the voters' and thirdly, a special session of Parliament to phase out the last white Parliament and ring in the new had to be held.

There is a standing committee of Parliament called the Standing Rules and Orders Committee. Its normal function is to oversee the proper working, debate and proceedings of Parliament in terms of a set of Rules and Orders agreed on and adhered to by all parties. One of its most important tasks for the 1984 session was to draw up a new set of Standing Rules and Orders for the new Parliament which would become operative at a special session of the last white Parliament later in the year in September. The Standing Rules and Orders Committee was one of the most senior, if not the most senior committee of Parliament, and on it served the Prime Minister, some senior Cabinet Ministers, the Speaker and leaders of other political parties. Put simply, we had to work out the rules of the political game in Parliament within the framework and dictates of the new Constitution. The practical workings of the new constitution were going to be far more complicated and difficult than anyone had really anticipated. Finally, at no stage in the proceedings of the new Parliament was the Nationalist Party as the dominant party going to relinquish its dominance and control. We had to listen solemnly to justifications of why it was in order to have joint sessions of all three Houses, but no joint debates, whilst on the Standing Committee on which all three Houses had representation there could be joint sittings and joint debates, but no joint decisions, and so on and so forth.

During the final weeks of July we debated the report of the Standing Committee on Rules and Orders. I had moved about twenty-one amendments together with about the same number from some of my colleagues. There was a general air of impatience with us from all sides of the House. It was felt that we were unnecessarily delaying the inevitable. The final Friday evening we were going to debate until the early hours of the morning. At about twelve-thirty am a senior Nationalist front bencher slid in next to me on my bench and wanted to know why I was being so bloody-minded. I patiently explained to him that I had some serious reservations about the practical working of the new Parliament, and that in any case most of my amendments were consequential to three substantive ones being accepted. If they were not, the others would fall away.

He listened to me quite intently, then shrugged resignedly and said, 'Any case, *die blerrie ding gaan nie werk nie*'. ('In any case, the bloody thing is not going to work').

That more or less summed up what I had tried to say during the referendum and I thought it a sad, but nevertheless appropriate comment from the last white Parliament in its dying moments.

In the meantime, the white euphoria of the referendum was followed by the signing of the Nkomati Accord on 16 March 1984, and the 'triumphant' return of the Prime Minister from his European trip. I thought the Nkomati Accord was a welcome development away from the posturing and clandestine destabilization that was going on. Sitting on the banks of Nkomati in the sweltering sun listening to P W Botha and Samora Machel extol the obvious virtues of good neighbourliness and mutual co-operation over that of hostility and confrontation, I could not but think back to 25 April 1974 when the coup took place in Lisbon that precipitated Machel's victory. Particularly, I recalled the excitement and expectation it had caused amongst our own 'black consciousness' people. They saw this as exportable revolution and some of them were arrested at Curries Fountain in Durban for holding a meeting which led to Pitman defending them in court and the SASO nine being sentenced to Robben Island. I looked at the small figure of Machel and thought how ironic it was that after about the same period those SASO youngsters had been sentenced to imprisonment he was signing a peace treaty with the same Government they had been hoping to overthrow – and he desperately needed that treaty. After the ceremony, under an oven of a tent, the Prime Minister called me towards him and Machel to introduce me.

I congratulated the Prime Minister on the success of the occasion and he formally introduced me to Machel by saying, 'You see, I talk to my Leader of the Opposition!'

He had a small point there somewhere.

There can be little doubt that the Nkomati Accord opened the way for the Prime Minister's visit to Europe. The official media treated it almost as the return of Christopher Columbus. Everyone felt his visit was quite an event, but nobody could put their finger on why it should be a good thing. The success of the trip lay in the fact that it had taken place at all; some hoped something good would rub off from the breaking of such prolonged isolation; others that he would tell them 'what it was really like' in South Africa. Whatever the case, he returned well pleased with himself and in a way it was also the end of the post-referendum honeymoon.

After that, things started going sour at quite a pace.

In August 1984, the Coloured and Indian elections took place and from every perspective they were an unmitigated disaster. Overseas they were regularly described as the 'sjambok' elections, with TV viewers seeing policemen whipping and chasing those who were against the elections. This soon dispelled any advantage – from a publicity or image point of view – of the new constitution being a 'step in the right direction'. One foreign editorial after the other reflected disillusionment and astonishment. Instead of the Government accepting it as a right of those who wished to boycott the elections to do so they started hounding them as revolutionaries and subversives. They simply would not understand that the one thing you cannot fabricate in politics is legitimacy.

The United Democratic Front (UDF) was a direct response to the introduction of the new constitution. There is no doubt that as a populist movement against the constitution this movement has been remarkably successful in a very short space of time. Its success is also due in no small measure to the heavy-handed approach of the Government. I do not accept that the low percentage poll in both elections is entirely a reflection of the support for the United Democratic Front, but it certainly could claim the propaganda victory; whereas those who were elected were on the defensive and laboured under credibility crises right from the outset. They certainly did not look like warriors who were going to dismantle apartheid from the inside, and who had the complete confidence of their respective communities.

This was very apparent when we parliamentarians gathered together for the first time in September 1984 to herald in the new Parliament in an extraordinary session. There were some orientation lectures for any who wished to attend, but of course, particularly for the new boys. I was asked to talk about the 'role and function of the Leader of the Opposition' in the new Parliament. During question time, it became embarrassingly obvious that the majority of those present did not have the vaguest idea of how the new constitution was going to operate.

One Labour Party MP in particular, Jac Rabie – who during the election campaign had made vicious and petty references to me and the PFP about our 'paternalism' and predicted how the Labour Party was going to take over 'our role' – could not understand how I still had the temerity to call myself the Leader of the Opposition, now that the Rev Allan Hendrickse had twice as many seats as I had. I tried to explain that the position of Leader of the Opposition was a constitutional and not a self-inflicted honorary one, and that in any case, Allan Hendrickse was constitutionally part of Government and not of Opposition, but it still seemed to escape him. Another, when I explained the consequences of collective Cabinet responsibility, wanted to know from me in front of everybody whether I thought it a good thing that Labour Party members should accept Cabinet positions!

The significance of the fact that we were experiencing the death rattle of the last white Parliament in Africa did not penetrate our proceedings. Despite the obvious official attempts to load the occasion with profundity the process was profoundly unimpressive. For the majority outside it was a big yawn. For those inside, it was a series of deeply undemocratic constitutional manoeuvrings. First, an electoral college was constituted which excluded all opposition parties in all houses from it and loaded the vote blatantly in favour of the Nationalist Party.

It then proceeded to elect a new President (guess who?) with the Coloureds and Indians not even bothering to nominate their own or oppose the one proposed: the argument being that it would have been only 'token opposition'. (Presumably, opposition only starts when you know you can win!) Then the Speaker was elected by the same electoral college in equally unanimous fashion. After that, there was the inauguration of the new executive State President in the Groote Kerk in Cape Town. Jonas Savimbi of UNITA was flown in and he and the Vice-President of Taiwan were the major foreign dignitary attractions for the occasion.

For the rest we were burying the last white Parliament on our own amidst the familar tinkling of our own medals and starched uniforms. I had always had a vision of the demise of the last white Parliament as a major event which would be of enormous symbolic significance. The whole wide world would be glued to this extraordinary moment when an embattled white minority would have successfully broadened the base of political participation in such a manner that a new era of negotiation politics away from racial hostility and confrontation would have begun. At least some enthusiasm from black, Coloured and Asian South Africans could be legitimately expected if such a broadening was successful. Instead, 319 of us snuggled and squeezed into the old House of Assembly of the old white Parliament to listen to the new State President make his first speech in the new 'non-white' Parliament.

The most amusing thing for me was the obvious discomfort and disgust on the faces of the Conservative Party members and even a fair number of Nationalist MPs as well, when the Coloured and Asian MPs solemnly marched in and started taking their seats for the President's address. He read through an uninspiring speech in which the most significant point was that the most important unfinished business on the political agenda was that of black constitutional development. (Ah so! as our Japanese friends would say.) He marched out, we followed him, and the first session of the new Parliament of the Republic had begun. It lasted only a few more days.

We, the PFP, tried to prolong it by moving two motions: one to discuss, by means of a special motion of public interest, the alarming state of the economy; the other, to discuss the state of escalating unrest and instability in the black townships. The first the Speaker granted and this led to a two and a half hour debate. The second was prevented by the Leader of the white House moving an adjournment. So we all trooped out to return in January 1985 for the first full-length session of the new tri-cameral Parliament.

What is to be done?

This question is, of course, the title of a famous pamphlet written by one Vladimir Iliyich Ulyanov, otherwise known as Lenin. He wrote it before the 1917 Revolution at a time of great confusion in the opposition ranks in Russia. There was bickering and squabbling, moral outbidding on a grand scale, and everyone had his own idea of what should be done and which strategy would succeed in changing the social and political order. Lenin's own suggestion was the formation of a party of professional revolutionaries, limited in number but highly centralized – 'the dictatorship of the proletariat' – that would stage-manage the workers' revolt as soon as conditions were favourable. Anyone who has read an account of that turbulent period in Russia's history cannot but marvel at the coincidences that surrounded the fortuitous success of Lenin's answer to his own question. Despite the fact that since then unsuccessful revolutions have outnumbered successful ones by an impressive margin, many have continued to believe that Lenin's recipe was not only exportable to other countries, but even guaranteed success.

In borrowing Lenin's question for South Africa, I run the risk of being presumptuous. South Africa is not Russia, and Slabbert is most certainly not Lenin. I have been jokingly compared, by Heribert Adam, to a third-rate Kerensky, but even that is too flattering for someone who lacks the dogmatic confidence and sense of destiny they both displayed with *élan*.

But Lenin's question is interesting, especially for South Africa. And when I ask it, I do not do so rhetorically, as Lenin did, because he had a simple and exclusive answer to it. I do not believe such an answer is available for South Africa (or ever has been for any country really; but that is a philosophical debate for another occasion.) I pose this question so that I can take stock of the answers that have been given to it over the period that I have been serving in the last white Parliament, and perhaps even a bit before. I believe that the manner in which groups, movements and individuals pursue the realization of the various answers will in all likelihood determine more accurately what is going to happen in South Africa rather than what any single individual or group believes or thinks should be done. The plans and actions of one must necessarily affect those of others and vice versa. After all, no domination is eternal, nor are revolutions entirely successful, and political engineering on a grand scale is notorious for under- or overestimating the use of social means to achieve political ends. This inescapable fact of history has not deterred people from time and again repeating Lenin's question, and in many cases, having their answers ready in their inside pockets before actually asking it.

This is also the case for South Africa. For my own clarity, I will try to identify the assumptions, strategies, and actions which have been involved in answering the question: 'What is to be done?' Of course, I cannot escape relating myself to the question and those answers. After all, for my sins, I was the last Leader of the Opposition of the last white Parliament and have to give an account of what I, and others with me, have been trying to do in this regard.

The first general observation that is self-evident to me is that this is an instrumental question; 'done' to achieve what? In this sense, it is a strategy question in relation to some goal or set of goals. One thing that has always struck me about South Africa is that very often people using the same strategy have different goals in mind, and, even more likely, people with the same goals in mind use different strategies. A great deal of heat and energy is generated in defending or defining as out of bounds, one strategy compared to another. People become so vehement about the merits of a particular strategy, or the demerits of another, that the action in relation to either becomes a goal in itself. Of course, what makes it even more confusing is when people talk about the same goals, but have different things in mind.

My second general observation is that when it comes to goals, people are clearer about what they do not like than about what they would like to see replace what they do not like. Thus, most are agreed about the untenability of racist laws, influx control, domination and other identifiable concrete practices which affect them, but when asked what kind of South Africa they would like to live in, they either say one without racist laws, influx control, or domination, or they talk in the abstract about a just society where there is equality of opportunity and economic justice.

My final general observation is that although a minority may be politically conscious and active about the question, the average person is aware of certain popular end-game scenarios about 'what is going to happen?' rather than, 'what is to be done?' They create the climate within which a popular political culture thrives and which forms the background for the more serious 'what is to be done?' strategies. You can almost draw a distinction between white end-game scenarios and black end-game scenarios, but they do sometimes overlap. An obvious white/black one is 'there is going to be a blood-bath' or some variation of it. Some blacks say it to scare whites and some whites say it because of 'My God, if I were black I wouldn't take it' feelings. Another scenario is that white 'time is running out' with its black counterpart of 'history is on our side'. Whatever the specific idea behind end-game scenarios of this kind all of them have in common some cataclysmic event, occasion or moment which blacks popularly identify with liberation and whites with damnation.

I am desperately bored by this 'five-minutes-to-midnight-heavy-breathing' politics. Time and again I have sat in at dinner parties where some angry black has rolled his eyes at the assembled whites, promising the day of Armageddon and watched them get goose-pimples.

The other dividing line between one kind of strategy and another is the role of violence. There are those who have defined the situation in such a manner that they see violence as the only way in which it can 'really' be changed. A full-blown revolutionary situation or a state of civil war is one where violence becomes the pervading means on either side of the divide to either maintain or change the status quo. I do not believe we are in a state of civil war in South Africa yet. In other words, there is still sufficient flexibility or 'give' in the system for other modes of change to have a chance to succeed. But this is small comfort if those other modes are not vigorously pursued. As a matter of course Government can rely on the ordinary citizen's abhorrence of violence when persecuting those who use it to try to change the status quo. But there is a direct correlation between the extension of coercive government and the use of violence by those who experience such coercion and wish to react to it. This is so because those who experience such coercion experience it as violence from the State on their own persons and in this manner violence begets violence. The more Government prevents peaceful and legitimate protests; the more it uses arbitrary arrests and detentions, raids and intimidatory tactics, the more certain we can be that increasing numbers of South Africans, who are at the receiving end of such methods, will begin to define the domestic situation in such desperate and inflexible terms that violence will be seen as the only way out.

If the Government continues to be insensitive to or ignorant of the interactive relationship between coercion and violence in South Africa, it is likely that violence and counter-violence will become the dominant strategy between itself and those who oppose it. This will be a tragedy for all of us. I say this because I do not see such a situation being resolved by a successful revolution or a return to manageable racial domination. I cannot see a successful overthrow of the present regime or a transformation of the status quo by violent means. Those who propagate and promote this likelihood are victims of romantic delusion, whatever the legitimacy of their grievances and the intensity of their feelings about them.

Modern techniques of domination – and the technology of warfare and social control – have become more sophisticated and effective. This is so quite apart from other considerations such as the will to survive of a threatened minority, and organizational and logistical problems. I have yet to come across any revolutionary analyses that can provide a plausible account of how an armed struggle is going to resolve itself successfully in favour of those on whose behalf it is claimed to be waged. In other words, I believe that the very attempt to bring about a 'successful' revolution will fundamentally destroy the societal resources necessary to re-establish an effective post-revolutionary government. At crucial stages in the account there is a withdrawal into tautological assumptions about the impact of external isolation together with the numerical disproportion between black and white; economic recession, the resilience of the labour movement. These assumptions can usually be countered by equally tautological ones from the 'other side', so that the debate becomes an academic one. For example, whites counter with 'their will to survive', that 'we have nowhere else to go and will fight to the end', 'military superiority', 'black division and ineptitude'.

At the same time I cannot see how those who govern can do so successfully by depending on coercive or violent measures. By successfully I mean, maintaining a working stability so that it appears that 'normal life' can carry on. The same kind of organizational problems which confront those who wish to promote revolution have to be faced by those who wish to prevent it. And, of course, the advantages of more sophisticated technology are not confined only to one side either. (Beirut provides chilling evidence of how even teenagers can use modern weaponry indiscriminately in urban warfare) The point I am making, of course, is that the use of inconclusive violence in a country such as ours is likely to end in siege.

Siege can last for a long time and we would do well to learn from countries such as Northern Ireland, the Sudan, Cyprus and Lebanon which are siege societies. A siege society is of course a warped society. All its resources; economic, physical and human as well as routine daily life become subject to siege: travel, architecture, leisure time activities are pervaded by concern about security and individual safety. The hallmarks of a siege culture are suspicion and mistrust, defining all situations and actions in terms of threat potential, a kind of 'us or them' approach to the future. In South Africa we are not quite there yet, but only the politically myopic would deny that we have already started on that road.

The final tragedy about violence as a strategy is that those who rely on it become immune to reason and the weight of factual evidence against its use. You can point out how unpredictable it is as an instrument to achieve the desired ends; you can wax eloquent on the horror and despair it causes and even advance the most compelling moral arguments against it; but those who have committed themselves to it, either to change or maintain the status quo, are victims of the questionable assumption that by using it they are 'teaching the other side a lesson' which will change its actions and convictions. In fact, more often than not, exactly the opposite happens, and the familiar spiral of violence and counter-violence is the consequence.

Another strategic dividing line on the 'What is to be done?' question in South Africa is whether one depends on 'outside' or 'inside' forces to bring about the final change. This division does not imply mutually exclusive strategies, but rather reflects a matter of selective emphasis. Thus, when one states that 'outside economic pressure' is the last hope for the black man 'otherwise he resorts to violence', one ascribes a great deal of causal significance to such forces in resolving the domestic conflicts of South Africa. The same applies when one advocates that isolation and boycott are the only options open to the 'world' in its response to the internal situation in our country.

What could possibly be the assumptions underlying the 'role of outside forces' strategy? Obviously it is assumed that if a powerful enough external factor acted in a particular way this would somehow (a) compel the South African Government to act in a desired way, or (b) strengthen those who struggle against it, in such a manner that a more desirable state of affairs for the 'oppressed' or 'suffering' would be the consequence. I think we must distinguish between two important issues in these sets of assumptions: the manner in which an external factor can act, on the one hand, and the kind of response domestically to such actions, on the other. These two issues cover a host of other unstated assumptions for which there appear to be very little supporting evidence.

Take the question of the manner in which an external factor can act. What would constitute such an external factor? I believe we can identify three broad categories: governments, business, and special interest lobbies such as Churches, sporting bodies and universities. In the case of governments it must be assumed that such action will be reflected in foreign policy. Hypothetically, if all governments shared the same abhorrence of the domestic policy of the South African Government and collectively decided on the same foreign policy action, it could have a significant impact on the South African Government.

Thus we heard of a total strategic fuel embargo, an international refusal of landing rights, withdrawal of communication and postal privileges. All this is premised on the assumption that governments, in the case of South Africa, would make an exception and base their foreign policy action on a shared moral rejection of apartheid or separate development and a desire to assist those who suffer from it to the exclusion of all other considerations. This is, of course, sheer unadulterated nonsense. I have yet to hear of any government that does not base its foreign policy approach on its own perceived domestic and internationally strategic interests. These differ widely among governments depending on their geographic location, internal resource base, size, spheres of influence and strategic significance to the super powers.

When talking about a government's strategic interests, it is as well to keep in mind that there are not only government to government relations, but government to business or private sector relations with other countries as well. A government's need for some strategic raw material or commodity weighs stronger than questions of morality or strategies of a punitive kind towards other governments.

Thus, although Moscow is perceived by the South African Government to be the arch foreign enemy, there appears to be reasonably easy communication between it and private sector interests in diamonds here in South Africa. Trade between the latter and neighbouring African states, who presumably abhor the system in South Africa as much as any other country, is also palpably evident.

When it comes to business as an external factor, it surely does not need to be argued that there is no such thing as a collective international business ethic concerning the domestic affairs of any foreign country. Business pursues profit, not morality. Even if some business firms are more sensitive to domestic pressures concerning foreign investments, there is abundant evidence that if there is profit to be made and for whatever reason some withdraw, others will take their place. At this very moment most of the relief food for the starving multitudes in Ethiopia does not even reach its destination, but is being bought and resold in the domestic market. As far as I am concerned, I prefer a foreign company sensitive to domestic pressure concerning fair employment practices in another country than one which is not. It is futile to rant and rave about the immorality of foreign firms 'buttressing a vicious system' by their involvement in South Africa.

In fact, if it is quite clear from available evidence that foreign governments and businesses are not going to act as prime movers in changing the domestic situation in South Africa, the morality of keeping alive the hope or the fiction that they can play such a role, is equally questionable.

Special interest lobbies as an external source of pressure are quite an interesting phenomenon. It would appear that their impact is more effective domestically than on a foreign target area. Thus, multinationals in the United States of America can sometimes find themselves spending a disproportionate amount of time explaining or justifying their small percentage of investment in South Africa. It also appears that foreign 'issues', such as apartheid for example, have a fluctuating relevance in those countries depending on the importance of other issues both internationally and domestically. Generally speaking, special interest lobbies sustain a kind of moral climate against apartheid and racism rather than concretely managing to change any specific policy.

For me, there is one very clear exception and that is in the area of sport. There is no question that the sports boycott was effective in bringing about changes. Ironically, however, these very changes are dismissed as inconsequential and cosmetic by those who believe that such changes could be brought about by external pressure.

One thing is clear, though: anyone who pursues the external factor as a strategy for internal change, will find a ready and enthusiastic audience with guaranteed media coverage precisely because of the institutionalization of such special interest lobbies overseas. 'Fighting apartheid from outside' has become a growth industry with its own bureaucratic needs and vested interests.

The other dimension to the role of the external factor which has to be considered can be put as follows: assuming that some external factor could be mobilized as effectively as possible, what would be the presumed beneficial consequences for resolving the internal problem in South Africa? As I have suggested, there appear to be two general answers: (a) The South African Government will 'come to its senses' or 'see the errors of its ways', or be 'forced to the negotiating table' or 'be sufficiently weakened to succumb to other domestic pressures'. The other side of the coin is never seriously considered, namely that the South African Government could become more repressive, more obdurate and less inclined to rationality. When it is considered, it is done in tortuous logic which argues that this is necessary because it 'has to get worse so that it can become better'. The one clear case of a reasonably successful external embargo somehow fails to impress those who persist with this kind of strategy. Through Armscor, South Africa is now almost self-sufficient in supplying its own weaponry and is successfully exporting arms. When I pointed out this anomaly to someone who had regularly drafted resolutions for international conferences in favour of an arms embargo against South Africa, he conceded that it did not make sense, but in the present 'moral climate' it would be 'suicide' not to support such resolutions. Somehow the means had become confused with the ends – the strategy had become the goal itself. (b) The second kind of answer is that somehow the blacks or 'oppressed' or those involved in 'the struggle' will benefit by the concerted action of an external factor. It is very difficult to pin down what specific form this 'goodness' is going to take. Examples vary from the argument that at least the outside world demonstrates its moral support 'for the oppressed', to the fallacious assumption that if the South African Government is deprived of commodity Y it will then spend its money on commodity X, which will be to the benefit of the blacks. For example, less money spent on Defence will mean more money spent on black education. This is an absurd assumption. The most far-fetched argument in this vein is that blacks cannot suffer any more than they are at the moment and therefore concerted external action will increasingly isolate the South African Government and weaken it. Eventually this weakening process must be to the benefit of the majority. The other side of the argument is, of course, that things can get considerably worse without getting better at all, and that relatively speaking, the South African Government can become stronger and even more coercive than it is at present.

Having listened to many arguments on the role of the external factor as part of the answer to the: 'What is to be done?' question, and having sat in on numerous conferences on how the outside world can help the inside world of South Africa, the following appears to me to be clear:

– All the evidence points to the fact that no external factor, be it Government, business or special interest lobby can be the major influence on internal changes in South Africa. Such a factor could play a precipitant, 'last-straw-that-broke-the-camel's-back' role, but only because of major internal developments.
– Again, evidence supports the conclusion that, to the extent that an external factor has tried to play a decisive role, the consequences have been counter-productive to the intentions, neither have 'the blacks benefited' in any tangible sense, nor has the South African Government been weakened. On the contrary, more often than not an increased sense of isolation and external moral condem-

nation has been repeatedly used with great effect by the South African Government to consolidate its support amongst whites and to foster a siege-like 'us-against-the world' mentality.

Despite the two points above, those who pursue the external factor strategy will have a ready market and audience overseas that will guarantee publicity out of all proportion to its domestic effectiveness. This attention is perhaps what persuades them to insist that somehow the 'outside' world has a special role to play in the 'inside' world of South Africa.

If an external factor is going to play a strategic role, interaction with South Africa is perhaps more effective than boycott. Once you have isolated and expelled something, you no longer have any responsibility towards it – you can forget about it and you may even feel better for being able to do so. The more South Africa has to interact with 'the world', the more it has to become involved and interdependent with that world, the greater the likelihood that the absurdity and untenability of apartheid will be exposed, and the more vulnerable the domestic situation will be to external pressures and changes. Generally speaking, I believe this to be so whether the external factor be a government, multinational business or special interest lobby. However, just as I am convinced that an external factor cannot play the determinant role through isolating South Africa, it will not be a prime mover by becoming involved with South Africa either. As I said, on the balance of aggregates the advantages of the latter outweigh those of the former. In the prevailing international climate of opinion about South Africa this would no doubt be dismissed as political blasphemy and an obvious ploy to prop up the system.

I suppose this is inevitable, if the logic that inspires this reaction insists that the best way to change something is to have nothing to do with it.

A variation of the inside/outside strategy does not refer to the country but to the system. A great deal of heat, emotion and political argument had been devoted to the question of whether or not you should be 'part of the system', and try to 'change it from within' or whether or not you should have 'nothing to do with the system' and try to 'change it from the outside'. The crucial issue becomes that of defining the boundaries of the system. When are you part of it through your action? Does your strategy support or undermine the system? Your definition and delimitation of the system usually reveals your own ideological predisposition and by inference the shortcomings of your opponents. If the system is seen to be 'exploitative racial capitalism' then anything which is related to the 'economic system' in the broadest sense, is 'part of the system'. Such a broad definition narrows down the range of non-systemic strategies to change. From my own brief experience of discussions of this kind, more time seems to be devoted to discussing strategies that should not be pursued than those that should.

If the definition of the system refers to racially exclusive structures, the strategy is to avoid participation in such structures. The mere fact of participation is interpreted as 'support' of the system and those guilty of doing so are looked upon as 'sell-outs', 'stooges' or 'collaborators'.

My own point of view is that the inside/outside the system controversy is a fruitless one when considering strategies for change. It concerns the arena of moral outbidding and puritanical one-upmanship. Whatever the ideological definition of the system it is difficult to see how someone can define himself out of the system or think of any meaningful strategy that does not have to engage the system in one way or another. If it does not engage, it becomes moral masturbation, a rationalization of inaction. Even the essence of a Marxist strategy to promote class conflict depends fundamentally on system participation. If not, what is the logic of the dialectic all about?

The question for me has never been whether we are part of 'the system' or not, but what we are prepared to do about it. I have been contaminated by laws I did not make ever since I became aware of my own intelligence. Because of the colour of my skin, I have been the beneficiary of the institutions created by those laws whilst others who do not legally share 'my colour' have been deprived. This is going to go on being the case until the system which generates those laws and those who dominate it changes. Any strategy which engages the system to this effect should be seriously considered in terms of its ability to apply pressure and bring about rational non-violent change. Why do I qualify with 'rational' and 'non-violent'? Rationality is important in the sense that it assumes some relationship between means and ends. It would be non-rational for me to substitute one totalitarian élite with another, or deliberately change the present system for a worse one.

Violence as an instrument of change, I believe, increases the unpredictability of the outcome and therefore the scope of non-rational action. It could be argued, and no doubt will be, that this is a conveniently smug position to adopt for a whitey in a racially dominated society controlled by others of his kind. That is an accident of history for which I refuse to accept blame or feel guilty. It does not blind me to the fact that totalitarianism, racial domination, exploitation and bureaucratic persecution do not depend purely on a white skin.

Any strategy which engages the system to bring about non-violent change away from racial domination and racial privilege should be seriously considered in terms of its ability to apply and increase pressure to this effect. That is why I also have no difficulty in deciding on the merits of so-called parliamentary or extra-parliamentary strategies for change. It is the present Government which has made it constitutionally impossible for the majority of the people subjected to its laws to consider parliamentary strategies for change. Therefore those thus excluded have no option but to consider extra-parliamentary strategies. It is pure hypocrisy and down-right provocation on the part of Government to equate all extra-parliamentary strategies for change with unconstitutional and even subversive strategies.

I have no difficulty whatsoever in understanding the formation of a movement such as the UDF, and even accepting the need for it. Constitutional or lawful extra-parliamentary opposition in South Africa is an inevitable consequence of Government policy and it is to a large extent Government reaction to such opposition which will determine whether or not it is forced into unconstitutional strategies. I do not understand why the UDF prevents some of its supporters who do have legal access to Parliament from making use of this. I find it difficult to accept the argument that, had the UDF won the majority of seats in the Coloured and Indian elections (which would appear to be possible if the support they claim for themselves in these communities is valid), this would have had no effect on the manner in which the new constitution was to be implemented or how it worked. Their argument for not doing so, simply falls into the quagmire of a *non sequitur* in the inside/outside the system debate, and I fear as long as this debate remains the major concern of the UDF and similar organizations, they will remain opposition movements in search of enduring political strategies. Up to now it would appear that all its major political actions have been determined by Government rather than by their own initiatives: opposition to the new constitution, the elections, Crossroads and police action on township unrest.

One important lesson to be learnt from the labour movement is that it has engaged the system to great effect – the black trade union movement may not like this to be said, but theirs is a prime example of using co-optive structures for pursuing consequences unintended by those who created them. They have effectively explored the dynamics of co-optive politics without being seduced by it. The successful political equivalent of this kind of economic action has yet to be found in South Africa.

For the time being, we are going to remain trapped in the futility of the inside/outside the system, extra-parliamentary/parliamentary action debate. It is a debate full of breast-beating, lectern-thumping proclamations, denunciations and condemnations. For most involved, and there are exceptions, it is a debate long on rhetoric and short on action. The kind of action which predominates is protest and symbolism. As I have said, such action has a necessary and legitimate role and could very well be a preliminary stage in itself bringing about change. But those who actually confuse it with bringing about change have what I call the Walls of Jericho approach to change: if enough people can be molibilized to walk around and trumpet against the citadel of apartheid and display intense moral anger the walls may begin to crack. I am afraid Jericho was a one-time affair. What distinguishes protest action from bargaining or negotiation action is institutional leverage. That is why protest action without institutional leverage will always be vulnerable to counter-repressive measures.

This does not mean that those who have institutional leverage are free from counter-repressive measures. Trade union leaders are still harassed and arrested, but at greater cost to the system than in the case of protest leaders. However, to have institutional leverage it is necessary to explore the contradictions of the system itself and to exploit the unintended consequences which flow from the actions of those who govern. But this is to engage the system, and we get back to the tired old debate. There is one point in this debate that has to be taken seriously. It is possible to be seduced by the 'perks' of institutional participation. A 'stooge', 'collaborator', or 'Uncle Tom' is not determined by the fact of participation, but by the manner. However, this dilemma is not peculiar to those who function in the system. You find 'fat cat liberators' and 'professional boycotters' living it up far away from the arena of battle as well. I know, I have met them.

I have discussed these strategic options independently of ideology or a political dogma of change. Any one of these strategies can function within the context of more than one ideology. Also, I believe that the average individual who becomes involved in a political strategy is inspired by reasons other than ideological coherence and consistency. For example, I doubt whether the supporters of the UDF or Afrikaner Nationalism share the same clarity of thought on the philosophy of the movement as the more prominent ideologues in either camp.

Despite valiant attempts to ideologize 'the struggle' in South Africa along class lines or to square up the big '-isms' in a polarized contest of capitalism vs socialism, the vast majority of people define the conflict in racial terms: racism vs non-racism; racial exclusion and discrimination vs non-racial inclusion and non-discrimination; white domination vs black subjugation or vice versa, and so on. This is not to deny that Utopian socialism has not gained ground among black political movements. To the extent that capitalism has been identified with apartheid and big business has been seen to 'tuck in behind' or 'collaborate' with Government, this is to be expected. But, I believe the question of de-racializing political and economic participation will first have to resolve itself in South Africa before, and if, the grander ideological conflicts come into their own.

Another point that has to be considered when discussing the above-mentioned problems of strategy, is that no strategy can be divorced from the socio-economic context in which it is played out. It is useful to distinguish between planned and unplanned pressures for change. The unplanned pressures for change are very often crucial in determining the effectiveness of planned strategies to bring about change. Thus, in South Africa, the birthrate, patterns of population migration, the effect of drought, urbanization, decrease in agricultural resources, international economic fluctuations, will have a profound impact on the plans and strategies of competing groups and movements in South

Africa, and, in particular, on the present Government and those who oppose its policies.

As a result of these unplanned pressures for change, I anticipate that three areas will become the focal point of strategies for change: Labour, Education and Constitutional Development. These three areas will become increasingly interrelated and urban-based. The most strategically placed agent in relation to unplanned pressures for change in any society must be its Government. Through its budget and policy measures it demonstrates its awareness of the impact of such unplanned pressures and in a sense sets the stage for other groups and organizations to act in relation to such pressures. For example, if the Government budgets in anticipation of an unrealistically high price for gold by misreading the international economic situation, the impact is felt right through society in terms of money available for education; housing and welfare. Similarly, if the Government ignores the reality of urbanization, it contributes to the problems of urban conflict and community disintegration. Thus the Government as a strategically placed agent for planned change can either anticipate or react to unplanned pressures for change. A reactive Government in South Africa will always be seen to be doing too little too late, no matter how solemnly it confesses the sincerity of its intentions.

Apartheid as an attempt to anticipate pressures for change in South Africa has unleashed so many unintended consequences that the Government is likely to be forced into reacting to unplanned pressures for change for some time to come. Any other group pursuing strategies for change, that does not weigh up its strategies against those of the Government, does not appreciate what it means to engage 'the system' in any meaningful sense. Whatever the eventual outcome in South Africa, a white minority Government will be an intimate part of the process that brought it about. Any strategy that does not take this reality into account must budget generously for disillusionment.

Well then, if I am so eloquent and erudite about the pitfalls of other strategies, what about my own? I remember walking the streets of Paris recently with Breyten discussing the 'What is to be done?' question when he interrupted me with: 'It is comfortable to rationalize your own inconsequentiality. You must not be afraid to ask big questions even if the answers are not readily available'. There is a truth there. You can spend so much time knocking down the answers to the 'What is to be done?' question, that you end up in effect saying that nothing can be done. You can contribute toward bringing about what you fear will happen, by doing nothing to prevent it. At least I can begin my own answer by declaring that such is certainly not my intention.

Nor do I, by questioning the effectiveness of a strategy, necessarily doubt the sincerity of those who pursue it. However, if a strategy has been pursued for more than two decades it is not unreasonable to assess its worth as well as to consider the sacrifices it has cost those who have committed themselves to it.

I began by saying that the 'What is to be done?' question is an instrumental one; that it assumes a desirable state of affairs that has to be brought about as a result of a particular strategy or strategies. What desirable state of affairs do I have in mind? I believe it is possible to do away with racial domination in politics; to get rid of racist laws from the statute-books; to create a fairer non-racial provision of social services, and to have more freedom of movement and bargaining in the economy for the majority of people than we do at present. If any one of these could be achieved, we would have a more desirable state of affairs, and if all of them, then a very much more desirable state of affairs. The present political and economic system is the major stumbling block to bringing about such a state of affairs and therefore, as I said, any strategy which can bring about a change in this system toward that state of affairs is worth considering. If, however, the desirable state of affairs is some 'total situation' where the 'democratic will of the people' reigns supreme in the polity and the 'forces of production' are 'controlled by the working masses' in order to ensure 'economic justice', or on the other hand, the 'total situation is 'a plurality of independent sovereign states bound together in a constellation' where 'self-determination' is guaranteed for 'own affairs' and co-operation ensured on 'matters of common interests', I am at a complete loss to prescribe any strategy or to describe what such a 'total situation' could conceivably be.

My desirable state of affairs should make it clear that I do not believe in some final 'total situation', nor do I think there is any acceptable grand theory of change whose laws simply have to be discovered and followed to bring about the most desirable state of affairs. I do not believe the follies of the present, or the past for that matter, form part of some inevitable convulsion of history, en route to a final grand destination. To put it at its pompous best, unlike Marx, the socialist, or Rostow the capitalist, I am not a teleological determinist. I do not know the secrets of some 'inevitable dialectic' or the 'stages of growth' away from exploitation or traditionalism.

Therefore, the first point I have to make is that there is no fulcrum strategy; no single formula. To me this is so obvious it hardly bears stating. Yet nothing has consumed more energy and creativity in South Africa than the debate on which strategy is better than any other to bring about change.

The second obvious point to me is that the usefulness of a strategy can change over time. What is effective now may become obsolete tomorrow or vice versa. Therefore, to use a strategy at present that you ignored previously need not be a 'betrayal of principle' but simply good common sense in pursuing a desirable state of affairs. It is unfortunate, but almost endemic, that in South Africa personalities, prejudices, factions and movements have become bogged down and married to related strategies and arguments to the exclusion of the goals they were supposed to achieve. This is not to deny the relevance of arguments about principle. To be flexible about strategy does not mean that everything is possible and nothing is necessary. However, to be sensitive to matters of principle certainly does not mean being rigid and inflexible on matters of strategy.

I have suggested that the next decade or so will see strategies for change focus on three particular areas: Labour, Education and Constitutional Development. Obviously I do not exclude other areas as well, but I do believe that insofar as the unplanned pressures for change, such as population increase and urbanization, gather momentum, political strategies of planned change will manifest themselves in the organization of labour, the provision and structure of education and in the nature of constitutional development. Labour and Education will inevitably become increasingly politicized the longer it takes for adequate constitutional channels to develop. Anyone who does not see that black labour and education have become even more politicized in the months following the implementation of the new constitution, is out of touch with current trends.

In considering the strategies that will be prevalent in these three areas we must anticipate the reaction of the Government. Any strategy for change is an interaction between those who wish to bring it about, and those who resist such change. It is also an interaction between those who resist such change. In all three areas the Government can act seeking either confrontation or negotiation, using either repressive violence or dialogue. Similarly, those who pursue strategies for change in these areas in relation to Government can also promote confrontation or negotiation, using violence or dialogue. Over the next ten years it is more than likely that South Africa will experience violent confrontation, protest and constitutional change. In all three areas we will hover between becoming a siege or a co-operative society. There is no inevitable progression (regression?) to either. It is possible to learn from mistakes and it is also very likely that people do not. In either case it depends very much on what people do.

Obviously I would prefer it if we could move more and more to a co-operative society and away from a siege one. Therefore I favour negotiation strategies whether in the area of labour, education or constitutional development. Also, I believe it is possible for any individual to become involved in such strategies in these areas. However, a particular responsibility rests on whites to promote such strategies in the constitutional field because for so long they have monopolized the institution which has to initiate constitutional change, namely, Parliament. For me it is both ironical and a matter of deep concern at the end of the last white Parliament that the new one in terms of its composition, structure and political philosophy does very little to promote the possibility of real negotiation politics in the area of constitutional development. In fact, it could make it more difficult. But that it remains necessary to try and promote such politics is for me beyond question. That is why I have no difficulty trying to explain why I am in Parliament and what I am trying to do and why I am encouraging others to do the same. I do have difficulty in assessing with confidence how successful my strategy has been or the chances of its being more so. As our society lurches between siege and negotiation so our mood shifts from despair to hope. And so it is going to be for quite some time, I imagine.

But if I have to do some dispassionate crystal ball gazing in the field of constitutional development, I see the outlines of a picture.

The most important constitutional shift with the demise of the last white Parliament has been a shift of co-optive politics towards the political centre. Because this shift has only included the so-called Coloured and Indian minorities it has highlighted the absence of similar co-optive structures for blacks and also underlined the hopeless inadequacy of existing constitutional structures for effective negotiation politics. The Government can either insist that co-option to the centre is only limited to Coloureds or Asians (in which case we can prepare for siege and confrontation between black and non-black), or else the Government can initiate some process to bring about black co-option to the centre, in which case we *may* move towards more co-operative constitutional development.

I believe at the moment that those who wish to initiate co-optive politics towards the centre for blacks are rising in the key areas of National Party domination. I have no idea what kind of structures may emerge – I find the idea of a fourth chamber for blacks in a tricameral Parliament totally ludicrous – but of two things I am certain: if those new structures are to stand the slightest chance of promoting negotiation politics in the area of constitutional change, they will be urban-based and they will fall outside the conventional logic of homeland separate development. If this does happen, I hope that those who pursue non-violent strategies for change would examine those structures very carefully to exploit their possibilities and contradictions. Whatever others may say about someone like Gatsha Buthelezi (of Inkatha) I cannot fault the logic of his strategy in exploring the dynamics of the limited co-optive structures at his disposal.

It must be kept in mind that those structures had no access to the centre and were rural-based. Even so, he has managed to establish an impressive power base of constituency and accountable politics. The shift of co-optive politics towards the centre and the urban areas has determined the arena where the options of siege or negotiation will play themselves out in the area of constitutional development over the next ten years or so. I am afraid it is going to be painful.

So much for my reflections on Lenin's question. Not very cheerful and earth-shattering, I must agree. But after ten years in the last white Parliament, I believe it to be immoral to dispense easy optimism in a country such as ours. It is far easier to understand change than to bring about 'a desirable state of affairs' through one's strategies. My optimism has been shaped and modified by my own limited attempts and my interaction with others who also have their strategies and hopes. When I look towards the future, I am fearful of the long darkness that may await us all. I am saddened by the human potential we have squandered and by how we have participated in our own brutalization. But we here in South Africa have problems to solve for which the rest of the world has found no solutions and that in itself is a great challenge. We have the potential and the opportunity to break new ground. The most devout wish for the future I can express for our land and its people is that we proceed by avoiding the mistakes committed by others and ourselves in the past. Being human, of course, that is never easy.

'The future is not what it used to be'

One evening in the House of Assembly, Major Ruben Sive paraphrased this quote from the French poet, Paul Valery, to polish his point that the plans of the Nationalist Party had gone awry. There is no better way to sum up the mood that prevailed in Parliament and the country when we came to the end of the first, full-blown session of the tri-cameral infant which was spawned by the last white Parliament.

Are we heading for siege or negotiation? During this session on the positive side:

The State President gives up on the homelands policy as the final solution; promises to look again at the issue of black citizenship and influx control; says he wishes to negotiate with all black leaders who reject violence; is prepared to create an informal forum to discuss 'a wide range of constitutional issues'; offers a conditional release to Nelson Mandela and other political prisoners; invites opposition parties to participate on an enlarged cabinet council to assist in finding consensus on negotiation. At the same time the Immorality Act (Section 16), the Prohibition of Mixed Marriages Act and the Political Interference Act are repealed and thus voluntary association is restored to sexual intercourse, marriage and party political membership on a non-racial basis.

All this is new and quite extraordinary in terms of conventional Nationalist Party politics.

Yet also during this session on the negative side:

Mandela rejects the offer; no significant response is forthcoming from the ANC, UDF, black trade unions or Inkatha to the State President's initiatives. The general reaction seems to be: 'So what, tell us more'. Urban unrest escalates. People die in confrontations with the police all over the country, but in particular Crossroads, Langa and Kwanobuhle grab international headlines. The Kannemeyer report on the Langa killings paints a frightening picture of

144

police indifference to conventional methods of riot control. Since the SADF has been deployed to deal with urban unrest, it has been responsible for five deaths. UDF leaders have been detained; some charged with treason. The State President is adamant that he will maintain law and order at all costs. The SADF raid deep into Northern Angola, near the Cabinda oilfields, ostensibly to gather intelligence on ANC, but very few accept the credibility of this official explanation. Especially after the Minister of Foreign Affairs, Pik Botha, quite blandly tells Parliament that the SADF had been supporting RENAMO (a rebel terror group in Mocambique) prior to the signing of the Nkomati accord on 16 March 1984; also that Parliament has been deliberately uninformed and, if necessary, the Government will do the same again. Bombs are thrown into the houses of two MPs (House of Representatives). This is followed by an SADF raid into Gaborone, Botswana, in which twelve ANC members and friends are killed. Indiscriminate violence being met with indiscriminate retaliation. The economy is down; inflation and unemployment up. The disinvestment campaign has gathered momentum – South Africa is a free kick for every group seeking to broaden its domestic support base; from well-intentioned special interest lobbies to weirdos on the lunatic fringe.

What do we make of all this? There is a current myth doing the rounds amongst some of the shakers and movers in the establishment, called 'the Huntington thesis' (after an American political scientist who expounded his version of it in South Africa during the referendum build-up. Somehow the myth has outgrown Huntington himself). According to this thesis we should not be worried about the apparent paradoxes; coercion and reform go hand in hand; a measure of instability is a symptom of successful reform. Some even hint at a grand plan, where all the above contradictions are resolved. We lesser lights are cast in pre-ordained roles; we fit snugly into a government controlled hidden agenda.

Forget about it.

The only thing that is clear is the confusion. Long before mandarins of the Press and the Establishment were beguiled by the 'Huntington thesis', with the idea of 'reform by stealth behind an authoritarian façade', Machiavelli had explained it better in *The Prince*. If this Government really wants to bring about effective reform, it is going to have to get some heavyweight customers into the workshop. As long as it fails to understand why it does not have those customers now, it can forget about support for its initiatives, no matter how much some incant Huntington. Successful reform is a two-way street. The best evidence of it working is the other side's commitment to it.

The first six months of '85 have been the most absorbing of the eleven years I have been in Parliament. The above-mentioned symptoms of seige and negotiation are also signs of underlying structural changes that are taking place. The impact of stepped-up black urbanization is only beginning to show. It is an irreversible trend with far-reaching implications for the way we plan housing, residential and community development. Our cities are going to look completely different in ten years' time. Our economic recession is not just a cyclical affair that can be corrected by a favourable gold price and good weather. Fiscal and monetary tinkering cannot disguise any longer that we have an enormously expensive and wasteful State policy; that we have, comparatively speaking, a very unproductive labour force for a competitive industrial country and that our entrepreneurial base is too shaky and small to be the sole 'engine room' for growth. Our economic recovery is going to require some far-reaching *political* decisions, before and if, it is going to come about, decisions concerning freedom of association and organization in the market place; the provision and quality of training and education; the availability and disposability of land for residential and other purposes. Constitutionally, however, we are inadequately prepared to take, or administer, such decisions. Therein lies the special challenge of this period of transition: we have to search for the constitutional instruments that should already be available to meet the changes taking place.

I use the words 'we' and 'search' deliberately. This year I have spoken frankly and informally to MPs from all the parties; a few times to the State President, as well as to Cabinet Ministers. Outside Parliament I did the same with corporate and business leaders, academics, Bishop Tutu, Dr Nthato Motlana, black community leaders from townships torn by riots and confrontations with the police; members of the UDF, ANC, Inkatha and Chief Buthelezi; heads of the SADF, Police and National Intelligence Service (NIS). Almost without exception, for whatever ideological reason, there is acceptance that the existing constitutional, social and economic situation is untenable;

146

that there is real potential for lasting tragic conflict and that some way has to be found to avert it. For me, one of the most hopeful signs in our desperate situation is that such a diversity of (even hostile) interest groups agree on the need for change to avoid tragedy and are applying their minds to it. If intention and motivation were all that mattered, that way would easily be found, but we are trapped in the structures of our past and live in pockets of ignorance of each other's problems, abilities and convictions. But more than that, different conceptions of power and privilege are involved, as well as what is negotiable and what not. I still believe a way can be found.

Why does Paul Valery's 'the future is not what it used to be', have an evocative appeal for me? Some impressions of '85:

P W Botha: He remains a political enigma; a mixture of sentimentality and intolerance. Since he became Prime Minister and State President, the softer side has prevailed. In the beginning of my political career I was often at the receiving end of his darker side. The ferocity of his vindictiveness and irrationality, when angered, never failed to amaze me. Now things appeared to have calmed down between us. He is disarmingly frank about his lack of analytical ability on complicated constitutional and economic affairs, but through years of practical experience in Government has developed the capacity to identify a crisis with unerring accuracy. And he is not afraid to deal with it. Courage is a rare phenomenon in politicians and he sometimes even has the courage of his ignorance. That is why it fell on his shoulders to break Afrikaner political unity; to sacrifice white exclusivity in Parliament; to abandon key principles of Nationalist Party ideology. His political instinct told him that to pursue the old road would deepen the crisis of Government, even if he did not know where the new road was or where it led. He initiated the search we are involved in and he is going to receive very little gratitude from the hard right or left for it. The right will vilify him for selling out the whites; the left for trying to buy off the revolution. (Both are wrong. The whites have not been sold out by a long shot and there is no revolution to buy off.) They are also wrong in the sense that P W Botha has little patience with grand ideology. He is essentially a crisis manager. His political philosophy is remarkably uncomplicated: if things go wrong, there must be an enemy responsible, and if they go right it is because of 'good Government'. The simplicity of the total onslaught philosophy appealed to him as Minister of Defence and he carried its logic into his office as Prime Minister and State President. If all else fails, Moscow must be responsible for what goes wrong, whether it be regional instability or domestic unrest, and those who do not accept this, are the witting or unwitting tools of it.

He is sincere in his willingness to consult with blacks and he intuitively recognizes how important the issue of citizenship is for them. But I do not think he really understands black politics and the issues that are central to it.

Too often there is a simplistic division between 'good' blacks who want to co-operate and 'terrorists' and 'communists' like 'the ANC and UDF'. It is to his credit that he is prepared to recognize the untenability of the present constitutional arrangements for blacks and is prepared to discuss alternatives. Yet emotionally, as well as intellectually, he cannot seem to accept a common constitutional arrangement between black and white.

He feels that for someone in his position he has gone as far as is necessary in politics in his country, and (correctly), that he has taken risks that others before him would not have contemplated. The tradition of Afrikaner leadership, from which he is drawn, values loyalty and obedience above all else. Temperamentally he is not suited to the style of negotiation politics, but insists on promoting it. The imperatives of time and metabolism are preparing him and the country for political transition, precisely when his initiatives are beginning to generate more confusion than clarity. Perhaps this is preferable to the predictable boredom of the past. He has contributed his bit to ensure that the future is not what it used to be.

Langa: On 21 March 1985 the police shot and killed twenty people from this Eastern Cape township. They were part of a crowd walking toward a funeral, which they thought was going to be held in another township. We in the PFP were busy with our weekly caucus meeting when Molly Blackburn, one of our Provincial Councillors from that area, and very much involved with black community affairs, phoned through from Uitenhage, the town near where the shooting took place. It was decided that six of our MPs would go there immediately to find out, as best they could, what had happened and I would seek an urgent interview with the State President.

148

He received me promptly and courteously. I urged him to use his influence to keep the police away from funerals and did not go into the townships unless absolutely necessary. It was too soon for him to know exactly what had happened, but he made it quite clear that he would maintain law and order whatever the costs and then read me a statement which his Minister of Law and Order subsequently read in Parliament an hour later as the official version of what had happened. The following day some of our MPs gave me preliminary accounts of what had actually happened on the day. These bore very little relation to the official version of the Minister and when the Press approached me I called for his resignation. The State President was furious. I was away campaigning in Natal when I received a message to call him. He accused me of 'jumping on the political bandwagon' (which one I don't know, as my party's stance was certainly not going to win us votes in the current by-election in Newton Park, in the Port Elizabeth area); of condoning the murder of 'responsible' township dwellers and the 'dancing on corpses' (a black community councillor had been hacked and burnt to death, apparently for collaborating with the police and exploiting people); and said that our relationship could not continue as before. I sensed another freeze setting in, but did not take it too seriously and by the time I got back to Parliament he seemed to have settled down. In any case, the discrepancy between his Minister's statement and the facts must have made it necessary to appoint Justice Kannemeyer as a one-man judicial Commission of Inquiry into the shootings.

The inquiry was limited only to the Langa shootings of 23 March. This was a pity. Unrest was rife throughout the country and particularly in the Eastern Cape. MPs from my party had compiled dozens of affidavits about questionable police action in Craddock, Port Alfred and Port Elizabeth, which we had made available to the Minister of Law and Order, as well as the State President. According to our view a full scale inquiry into the background of the unrest, as well as attempts to maintain law and order, was necessary. Our demands were ignored until the Langa killings drew the headlines. There is no doubt that the PFP report and the prompt action in compiling it had played a major role in precipitating this inquiry.

By the time I went to Uitenhage on 24 April to talk to some black community leaders from Langa and to attend the proceedings of the

Commission of Inquiry, more people had been shot in that month than on the day of the march to the funeral. I was also campaigning in the PFP by-election in Newton Park. Driving from Port Elizabeth to Uitenhage I passed the townships. All along, at spaced intervals, armoured cars waited. (The previous night on television they were displayed as well – for most white viewers symbols of security, for blacks instruments of siege.) Paper and debris had blown up against the fences, behind which stood row upon row of box-like shacks. I pictured the position of a young black just finished with school – no job and no prospect of one – trapped by constitutional design in this township, or one of a dozen others. No matter how creative or enterprising he was, he was compelled to live life out in a place like this. No Cabinet Minister could get it over his lips to admit that he was an ordinary South African citizen living in that township and the Government's Economic Development Programme expected 60% of the 2.5 million unemployed in two years time to be black and between thirteen and thirty-nine years of age, finding themselves in similar circumstances. All political meetings were banned and any person or movement outside Government approved structures and organizations were harassed and persecuted. Final power lay with the bureaucracy spawned by the Department of Co-operation and Development, but in the Uitenhage area interaction with the authorities had been reduced to the uniformed riot police. They had an impossible job and showed it.

In a backroom of a Catholic manse in Uitenhage, three black community spokesmen talk to me about conditions before and after the shootings. One wears a green blazer with a badge noting prowess in amateur boxing. Around us witnesses for the Kannemeyer inquiry wander about and wait their turn to go to court.

The black priest is angry, his voice rises: 'They call us savages. Can savages arrange a funeral attended by sixty thousand without incident? If we are supposed to hate whites, why can a young white couple walk around freely, with their baby, at the funeral without feeling threatened? Why could we do it? Because the riot police left us alone.'

The other one warns that there is one black with the name of Claassen, who, if found, is definitely going to get killed. 'He has raped and connived against too many people in the township.'

150

There is no threat in his manner of speaking, only resignation about the inevitable. Time and again the attitude and actions of the riot police are criticized: 'Police are supposed to be keepers of peace; here they only bring death' and similar statements. I also find a distinction between ordinary (good) police and riot (bad) police at subsequent meetings of the same kind. Without exception they want ordinary police to remain in townships and help with crime prevention. I leave to go to the proceedings of the inquiry not quite sure what long term solution they have in mind and it is agreed that we should meet again.

We tip-toe into the courtroom as the judge gives the assurance that no witness will suffer any detrimental consequences for giving evidence. The gallery is packed with blacks straining not to miss anything. I have to leave for a meeting in the Newton Park by-election. It is a morning one at a private house; about thirty people, middle to upper-middle class. Blacks and the unrest dominate the discussion.

Over a cup of tea a man walks up to me, blue veins on his nose, his paunch cascading over his belt: 'It's all very well what you say, but look how they kill each other. I always say you can take them out of the bush, but you can't take the bush out of them.'

This profundity gets apprehensive nods from some around us. I imagine the closest this fellow has ever been to a black township is his own kitchen.

Back at Parliament I see the Deputy Minister of Law and Order and Defence, Adriaan Vlok. Our careers in Parliament started in '74 and we have a comfortable relationship. He listens attentively as I tell him of what I found at Uitenhage and Port Elizabeth: the total breakdown of communication; the hostility toward the riot police; the need for Government to break through its self-created bureaucratic barriers and find out exactly what is going on in the townships. He appears genuine in his concern and wants me to stay in touch and bring any specific complaints to him.

A month later, again in Port Elizabeth en route to Cape Town from Durban, I meet with members of the UDF and ANC, as well as two of the three I met in the Catholic manse. Molly Blackburn set up the meeting. She has done fantastic work in keeping channels of communication open. In our country this is not often appreciated; we prefer to live with our illusions and would rather destroy the messenger than listen to his news.

A young black acts as chairman and does most of the talking as well. He speaks with articulate, controlled anger; the odd cliché betrays his ideological predispostion. There are thirteen of them. I have no doubt that these people have more credibility and standing in the communities from which they come than anyone the Government is in touch with. How do I know? I am quite prepared to choose anyone of the thirteen, and let any Cabinet Minister choose his contact, and let us each walk with our partner, unprotected, through the township and see who comes out with his shirt on the other side.

The discussion covers much the same ground: arbitrary actions of the riot police; corruption and complicity of Community Councillors; total rejection of the Government's local government policy for blacks and increasing involvement of the SADF in controlling unrest. A statement is handed to me in which a youngster describes how some SADF men had conducted themselves in a shebeen in one of the townships. They are quite happy for me to hand it to somebody in Government. I talk to a man who served a number of years on Robben Island.

'Nobody is going to tell me that this is not my country as much as it is P W Botha's, or anyone else's in Parliament'.

I believe him.

After the formal part of the meeting, the young chairman engages me in debate on my, and my party's, participation in the tricameral system.

'Get out man; it's a farce propping up apartheid. Look at those stooges on the gravy train. They can't even represent themselves properly'.

I explain the difference between engaging and isolating the system; my own preference for constitutional change.

I ask him, 'What do I do if I pull out, as you say?'

'You join us.'

'And then?'

'Then we march on Pretoria.'

I smile at him and he laughs quietly at the lameness of his metaphor.

The next day is a Monday and I have a two and a half hour seminar with the management of the National Intelligence Service on possible constitutional alternatives for South Africa. All very civil, no debate, only 'points of clarification' and appreciation for my time. That afternoon the Defence Vote is on in Parliament. I draw Adriaan Vlok's attention and in the lobby hand him the youngster's statement about the SADF men in the shebeen. He promises to investigate and I say to him that if anything should happen to that youngster, I would be of no further use to him or anybody on matters of this kind, nor would I wish to be. He reassures me.

Two weeks later the Kannemeyer Report is tabled and debated in Parliament. Amongst other points, the learned Judge concluded that:

- 'Had the funerals for March 21 1985 not been prohibited, the incident would not have occurred.'
- 'The attitude adopted by the police towards the funerals of people who died as a result of police action should be reviewed as a matter of urgency.'
- '... blame for the deaths of the persons killed in the incident and for the injuries sustained by others cannot be attributed to the error of judgement, or the human frailty of any one person. Had the holding of the funerals not unnecessarily been prohibited on doubtful ground, there can be little doubt that the procession would have passed through Uitenhage without incident along the normal route from Lange to Kwanobuhle, which happens to pass through part of the town. Had proper equipment been available the gathering may well have been dispersed with little or no harm to persons involved. The recurrence of an incident such as this can only be avoided by ensuring that proper use is made of the machinery provided by Section 46 of Act No 74 of 1982, and that police who may have to enforce the observance of an order issued in terms of that section, or to disperse riotous crowds generally, are fully and properly equipped for their task.'

The Judge established that: 'of those killed 5 were females and 15 were males. Their ages vary from 11 years to 50 years. Nine of the deceased were sixteen years old and younger.' Also that: '35 of the total of 47 dead and injured were shot from the rear.' A fact which the Judge found 'disquieting'!

The Ministry of Law and Order, in its memorandum on the Judge's report, promised that police procedures on funerals would be 'reviewed', as well as procedures on riot control and a Departmental Board would be appointed to consider 'certain findings' of the Judge. During the debate on the report Government members attacked PFP MPs for compiling our own Report and giving evidence to the Commission. E K Moorcroft, MP for Albany, wrote up the report, having been into the townships and taken affidavits. He speaks Xhosa fluently. Peter Gastrow, MP for Durban Central, spent the entire time of the inquiry in court, briefed to appear as Advocate on behalf of the PFP. The Government members who participated simply reshuffled some conclusions, assumptions and findings of the Kannemeyer Report in their speeches and thanked the police for the important work they were doing. With the exception of the Minister and Deputy Minister, who went primarily to see how the police were coping, and perhaps the MP for Uitenhage, none of them had been to the townships. Certainly it did not sound as if any of them relied on information other than that contained in the report or from 'official sources'. Their audience of reference was either themselves, the police or the white voters of Uitenhage. As I listened to the debate I recalled those straining black faces in the courtroom; the angry voices in the Catholic manse and the discussion in the derelict building in downtown Port Elizabeth one Sunday morning. I thought of the Judge's report. How mutually exclusive and inaccessible can our situation become?

The Media's Business and Politics: This year the *Rand Daily Mail* died. Its death was directly attributable to corporate indifference and atrocious mismanagement. Those who wanted to save it, could not, and those who could, did not care. In a space of ten years a newspaper with a circulation of 120 000, losing just under R250,000, ended up losing R15 million. Top management sailed through this period with impunity and attributed this decline to every conceivable cause, from the advent of TV, to editorial policy, to specific editors and journalists. It was abundantly clear that the problem was a managerial and not an editorial one. Nothing was done about it until it was hopelessly late. An incredible performance by any standard.

If you wish to test racial or communal insulation in South Africa, take a black newspaper for a week and compare its contents to that of a white newspaper. You read about two different worlds. The *Rand Daily Mail* tried to bridge that gap. Its passing reinforces our ignor-

154

ance. A number of very good accounts have been written of the last few years before Rhodesia became Zimbabwe. A common theme in most of them is that of declining information, or even progressive disinformation, about events in that society. Vilification for acts of terror from the one side was matched by praise and glorification from the other, and vice versa. Eventually the insulation became so complete that on the very day of elections after Lancaster House, Rhodesian Military Intelligence was sending reports through to South Africa to the effect that Robert Mugabe stood not the slightest chance of winning. In fact I was in a lift in the H F Verwoerd building, opposite Parliament, when I overheard a Cabinet Minister on that day saying: 'Bishop Muzerewa is still ahead, but Nkomo is closing fast.'

Increasingly, here in South Africa, unless you make a conscious effort, you will know less about how the other half lives. This effort cannot come from individuals or isolated organizations if it is going to be of any consequence in breaking through communal and racial insulation. It will have to come primarily from the media themselves. In a diverse and even dispersed society such as ours, it is incomprehensible that there can be a conventional or collective view about anything. Through the media world we will have to learn that we can thrive on the excitement of our diversity, or go under by denying it. To reflect alternative, even hostile viewpoints on everything from art to politics will season the average South African's mind to tolerate differences and to live creatively with them. Nothing blunts the spirit more than those SABC editorials trying to prove that we are right because the whole world is wrong. We can be assured that just as there is a drift towards an establishment ideology reflected in newspaper, radio and television reporting, so it will be met by the developing of an anti-establishment ideology. Eventually the country becomes polarized, the media, competing orthodoxies claiming to represent the 'real South Africa'.

It is in the media world that politics and business inevitably intersect. A corporation may wish to argue, and most of them do, that when it comes to choosing between competing values, the value of profit must be supreme, but no corporation must delude itself that it can escape the political consequences of exercising that choice. Particularly in a changing and volatile country such as ours, where the values of press freedom, racial justice, the rule of law and freedom of association are constantly under scrutiny. Either these values are vibrant and prominent before, during and after a period of transition, or they are deliberately undermined or destroyed as a consequence of it. In either event the corporate world in South Africa will play a crucial role, whether it wishes to or not.

In South Africa, generally speaking, the corporate sector avoids political controversy whenever possible and, if anything, is quietly supportive of Government as a source of stability necessary for business. The conventional entrepreneurial approach to activities of a social or working nature is that they should be indulged in as a consequence of, and not despite, the successful pursuit of profit.

However, the corporate sector has been thrust increasingly into the political arena in South Africa as conflicts of interest have developed between corporate and political goals. In this sense corporate South Africa is more highly politicized than most private sectors in other free enterprise societies. Corporate funded organizations and associations, such as The Urban Foundation, The South Africa Foundation, Associated Chambers of Commerce, Federated Chamber of Industries, Die Afrikaanse Handelsinstituut, very often adopt quasi-political stances in opposition to declared Government policy on matters in the fields of labour, housing and even political and civil rights. The approach is generally one of backroom diplomacy and bargaining and the avoidance of overt political opposition. The Urban Foundation, in particular, has been very active and successful in this field and for many politically aware businessmen has become the functional substitute for overtly declared political support.

Increasingly, however, corporate South Africa is going to find itself in a cleft stick situation. Common sense makes it clear that if free enterprise is to survive in the long-term, its philosophy and benefits will have to become a way of life for black South Africa. At the same time business feels that the patronage of Government must not be offended in the pursuit of immediate short-term corporate activity. That is why it is not strange to find the same business leaders who secretly make contact with the ANC overseas, insisting that the present Government is 'the only one that can help us through'. My own view is that this kind of ambivalence poses a threat to both the short and long-term interests of free enterprise. Another way out of this dilemma is to consciously and openly support and expand a com-

156

petitive media industry. This will be far more rewarding than trying to put one egg into two baskets. The death of the *Rand Daily Mail* is not an encouraging sign in this respect.

The 'apartheid must go, but only P W can do it' paradox was a common one I came across in recent discussions with top leaders of commerce and industry. It was argued that nothing must be done to offend him; to make him feel ganged up on, or to make his 'battle with the right wing' more difficult. There is an immediate chill in the conversation if you suggest that maybe 'P W does not want to get rid of apartheid all that quickly'.

'What?' they say, 'don't you realize he cannot move faster because of his right wing?'

What Right-Wing Threat?: One person who does not appear to take the right-wing threat seriously in the electoral sense is the State President himself. This was certainly quite evident in the conversations I had with him on the issue. This threat has been manipulated with great skill by Government spokesmen and their supporting media. A Cabinet Minister laughingly told me: 'Come election time all we do is show Eugene Terblanche (the right-wing, jackbooted leader of the Afrikaner Weerstand Beweging), giving his Nazi salute on TV and your voters will flock to our tables in the northern suburbs of Johannesburg'.

What is the political substance of this threat? It has to mean that the potential electoral support of the right-wing parties must be such that they can win the majority of seats in the House of Assembly in the next general election. At this stage all the right-wing parties combined have never polled higher than 17% of white voter support and in the most recent poll they have slipped to 15.5%. Even now the Conservative Party in the House of Assembly has only contested and won two of the eighteen seats it represents. How then, can that percentage of electoral support be distributed over eighty-four seats to win control of the House of Assembly? It is obvious nonsense.

But another version of the right-wing threat argument circumvents the above facts. It is the potential of right-wing growth that is the real threat, and that potential lies inside and not outside the Nationalist Party. That is why the real right-wing will not declare its preferences in attitude surveys or opinion polls.

'P W is fighting against his own party in trying to get rid of apartheid!'

Two simple questions: How? Over what? I sat in Parliament this year hearing the State President announce his initiatives and it was quite apparent that members of the NP caucus were hearing that news for the first time. It is also quite clear that the NP caucus is playing a decreasing role in the process of decision making. The initiatives involved policy shifts that were far more fundamental for conventional NP policy than the announcement of the tri-cameral Parliament being a form of healthy power sharing, which led to the breakaway of the Conservative Party. And yet, not one member of Parliament, either through conviction or expediency, broke ranks to join the Conservative Party. Some of them, considered to be potential right-wing supporters, explained with convincing eloquence why it was necessary to get rid of Section 16 of the Immorality Act. Five years ago you would have sworn they would willingly have given their lives to preserve it.

All these arguments serve no purpose to those who *want* to believe there is a right-wing threat. I suspect for some the threat achieves two purposes at once: it helps to polish the State President's halo, and to appear to be opposing apartheid by supporting him. A classical no lose situation, in which the cake is saved by consuming it.

There are two emotive fears, often unstated, which help to rationalize a right-wing threat. One is the fear of a reversion to old style white tribal dominance; a call to blood that will reconsolidate Afrikaner political unity. This is the impossible dream of the right-wing groups such as the Conservative and Herstigte Nasionale Party. I say impossible because the socio-economic circumstances which brought about that unity in the first place have changed irrevocably. For example, how does a group re-urbanize en masse? These right-wing groups have strong 'cargo-cult' characteristics. They are a tribe experiencing the dislocation of modernization coming together at ritual intervals, hoping for a cargo ship to off-load the good things and take the bad things away. The Conservative Party has taken over the old style Nationalist Party policy and dreams of restoring Afrikaner unity and white dominance to its heyday under Dr Verwoerd and Mr Vorster.

One afternoon in Parliament, a Conservative Party MP was being

158

taunted and heckled by the Nats. He stalked out of the assembly in a rage, to return about an hour later. Helen Suzman, who shares a bench with me, was out at the time and he slid in next to me. We had had a few lengthy discussions on politics and constitutional change in the past. He shook his finger at the Government.

'You see those bastards? We are going to break them, I promise you that!'

He paused awhile, sneaking a sideways glance to his colleagues, and winked at me.

'But once we have broken them, you fellows had better take over, because our plans are not going to work either!'

Glory be, this boy is out of touch.

The other fear is that white political support can be concentrated around a *new* policy or philosophy of racial domination. This fear immediately gives a more enlightened aura to the *existing* policy of racial domination and makes it appear *not* right-wing. All recent surveys seem to indicate that this fear has no factual basis. The most recent survey is a massive study of the Human Sciences Research Council (HSRC), which indicates that: '60% of whites said they expected South Africa to be fully integrated in 20 years time; 14% stood for some form of segregation and only 4% for complete segregation'.

So, if there is no right-wing threat, why is the President not moving faster? Because he does not want to and does not believe it is necessary. I imagine the kind of constraint he is under would be something like the following: Co-operation and Development, under Gerrit Viljoen as Minister, might argue for the complete abolition of influx control, but Defence or Police would see this as a security risk. *Or*, if you concede on black citizenship, you have to concede on one constitution, so you prevaricate on both. *Or*, if you withdraw riot police out of the townships, you find the ANC declaring them 'liberated zones'. *Or*, finally, if you are going to get rid of apartheid you have to concede the untenability of white domination. A valid consideration may be our fear of right-wing violence but this is not the same as an electoral threat and has to be dealt with by different means.

I believe Herman Gilliomee, of Cape Town University, had it right first time: The Government is exploring ways and means of sharing power without losing control of it. As there are no models readily available to achieve this, it is going to take a bit longer than some fear and others hope for. But the search for this power sharing by Government should not be summarily dismissed, because it will undoubtedly unleash, and is already unleashing, a new political dynamic that has to be explored and exploited for achieving evolutionary change.

The Tri-Cameral Parliament: Is it working? It depends what you are asking. Yes, it is working as a functioning organization. Rules and orders have begun to structure a common ritual of performance and some procedural hiccups are being ironed out. Yes, in that it has introduced a kind of multiracial *bonhomie* and tolerance in an institution where very little existed before.

A non-racial seasoning of the minds is taking place at cocktails, in dining rooms and standing committees. Thus people who would not normally associate with members of another race group are subjected to an involuntary learning process. As is not uncommon when this occurs, an initial air of virtuousness and determined good neighbourliness prevails, which is not a bad thing in our circumstances.

But as an instrument to broaden democracy; to reduce racial polarization and hostility and to promote the politics of consensus in South Africa, the tri-cameral Parliament is a hopeless failure. The sooner we face up to it, the less it is going to cost us. Those of us inside can insulate ourselves into a mutual admiration society and do our 'look Ma, no hands' routine, but the fact is that this new Parliament has become even more remote and isolated from the rest of society than the last white one. Not one law has been repealed, or initiative announced, in this one that could not easily have happened under the old one and with much greater effect.

Some would say I am simply rationalizing my own and my party's stance in the referendum. There is overwhelming subsequent evidence to support this conclusion: not one black leader, spokesman or editor of any standing, whether moderate or radical, is prepared to give even a qualified endorsement to the tri-cameral system. His credibility would not last ten seconds in his own community. I know from personal discussions (and anyone can read their public statements), that had some Government initiatives been announced before the implementation of the tri-cameral system, there would have been a vastly different reaction from black spokesmen.

Dr Motlana, in the Landdrost Hotel earlier this year: 'You know, if

160

they had come with some of these local Government plans to the Soweto Committee of Ten in 1977, we would have bought them. Now we dare not touch them with a barge pole.'

Chief Gatsha Buthelezi has repeatedly made the point that as long as Government initiatives toward blacks are perceived as a quid pro quo for the exclusion from Parliament there is no hope of co-operation. In this regard, to dismiss Bishop Tutu, Dr Allan Boesak and Dr Beyers Naude as radicals, is self-delusional. But even if the Government perceives them as militants or radicals, then if the tri-cameral system was supposed to undercut such radicalism or militancy, it has achieved exactly the opposite. To argue, as the SABC sometimes does, that such militancy is proof that the broadening of democracy and reform is actually working, is a staggering contribution to disinformation. The tri-cameral Parliament has made the politics of negotiation more difficult, whatever the good intentions about 'steps in the right direction' may have been.

Has the addition of the House of Representatives or the House of Delegates facilitated black/white dialogue or constitutional consultation? How? Where? Is there one MP or leader in the so-called Coloured or Indian Chambers that can set up any meeting or interaction with one black spokesman of consequence? Who? When? Could any one of them go back to their constituencies and hold advertised public meetings to report back how they had 'fought apartheid tooth and nail' as they had promised? If so, how many and who came to those meetings?

Both from analysis and experience, I know that as long as the logic, assumptions and laws which underpin the tri-cameral Parliament remain the basis for constitutional change in our country, the politics of negotiation will never get off the ground. Any new act or policy announcement, calculated to extend the logic and philosophy of the tri-cameral Parliament to other tiers of Government, prepares us for siege and confrontation. The only useful purpose this tri-cameral constitution serves is to get rid of it. Just as the last white Parliament had to be used to bring about this one, so this one will have to be used to bring about one constitution for all South Africans, based on one citizenship free of statutory discrimination and racial domination. The inevitable logic of constitutional evolution is that a constitution must be the instrument to bring it about, no matter how warped or inadequate that constitution may be.

Participation in the tri-cameral system is necessary because I believe evolutionary constitutional change is both possible and desirable. There are those who would disagree with me, and I fear their numbers are growing. Extra constitutional change is always dramatic, even violent, whether by coup or revolution. Even worse is when a constitution is suspended in a period of inconclusive siege. Although I believe evolutionary constitutional change to be both necessary and desirable, I have no illusions of how difficult it is going to be. One comfort is that every time an apartheid law is repealed and its underlying philosophy attacked and exposed, the untenability of the tri-cameral Parliament will be high-lighted, for it is founded on such laws and philosophy. And as the untenability becomes more pronounced, so the need and urgency for effective constitutional change will increase.

Constitutional Change: Is the Government serious about it, as far as black and white are concerned? The short answer is yes. But on its own terms. Thus far the Government appears unwilling to accept that there can be mutually agreed upon terms for constitutional negotiation. At the same time it accepts the untenability of the existing constitutional arrangement for blacks. It epitomizes the dilemma of wanting to share power without losing any. I cannot see how it can be done, but I suppose the Government is going to try for as long as it can.

The arch exponent of this approach is the Minister of Constitutional Affairs, Chris Heunis. He has a forceful 'be reasonable, agree with me' style and often succeeds in passing off persuasion as negotiation. This helped him to get a limited degree of co-operation from the Coloured and Indian population groups in order to launch the tri-cameral Parliament. But so far he has not been very successful in getting any black leader or politician of consequence to sound enthusiastic about any of his constitutional schemes. I believe there are a few very straightforward reasons for this:

In the first place the Government is reluctant to come clean on a number of key issues – the release of Nelson Mandela for example. The Government uses the issue of the rejection of violence to play

162

politics, rather than release him unconditionally. It was quite prepared to release Toivo Ja Toivo of SWAPO without precondition and Samora Machel, who according to its definition was a bush terrorist and depended on Moscow, was good enough to sign the Nkomati accord with them. The Government stance on Mandela is unconvincing.

Another issue on which it prevaricates is South African citizenship for blacks. The Government is prepared to investigate, consult on, consider and even reconsider, but will not state unequivocally whether the NP Government accepts a black as a fellow citizen of South Africa. This is the absolute minimum condition to get any constitutional negotiation off the ground.

There is a similar ambiguity on scrapping the policy of influx control – on a day to day basis, unquestionably the most hated policy by blacks. The Government will not say clearly that a black man is as entitled as anyone else to move around looking for a job and shelter. Again: they will 'look at influx control'; 'some of it will have to remain', but the Government intends focusing on 'positive urbanization'. Who do they wish to impress with such evasive claptrap? I wonder whether the Government has ever considered how an intelligent black, born and bred in a city, must respond to a Government declaration that this black man is now, as a matter of formal Government policy, considered to be 'permanently urbanized'. When this was announced in Parliament, the Nationalist MPs regarded this as a major shift and concession in policy. For the average urbanized black this is no big deal and a straightforward fact of life. It would be unreasonable to expect him to overwhelm the Government with gratitude and co-operation, unless he is clear about the constitutional consequences of this shift.

Part of the ambiguity about getting rid of influx control, is a suspicion, not unfounded, shared by many blacks, that the Government is searching for some administrative device to distinguish efficiently between 'urban insiders' and 'rural outsiders' for constitutional purposes. This is a useless endeavour. The same problems encountered in trying to decide who must stay away from the cities arise when trying to decide who can stay in. As long as the Government thinks that a separate constitutional solution for urban blacks is possible, it will prevaricate on scrapping influx control. It refuses to accept that urban black is a demographic description and not a viable constitutional entity. I often wondered what would have happened if the old United Party Government had insisted on treating rural whites as a separate constitutional entity. There would have been a lot of unhappy farmers and *plattelanders* stirring the pot.

Because of the Government's fence sitting on the above issues, Ministers tend to keep both ears to the ground when confronted with questions on: one constitution for black and white and power sharing in that constitution. Few things can be more embarrassing to watch than Cabinet Ministers, as well as the State President, squirming and kicking for touch on straighforward constitutional questions. Sometimes, after Chris Heunis has been interviewed, one needs a mental panga to hack through the conditional clauses and hyperbolic verbiage in order to establish whether he has said anything. From personal encounters with him I know that he can be extremely lucid and must conclude that these public demonstrations of obscurity serve some purpose in the Government's constitutional approach. I fail to see what success it has had in inducing blacks to co-operate.

The second reason for lack of progress on black/white constitutional negotiation is a substantial one and relates to what the Government spokesmen call the concept of the group in a future constitution. Chris Heunis and I differ fundamentally on this point. The Government insists the group membership, whether racial or ethnic, has to be constitutionally entrenched. Thus, in the present tri-cameral Parliament you have no choice whether you want to vote for, or belong to, the House of Assembly (white), House of Representatives (Coloureds) and House of Delegates (Indian) and if you are black, by law you cannot have anything to do with any of them.

This compulsory group membership is unilaterally determined and legally prescribed by the white minority. The latest research report of the HSRC has shown conclusively that this approach of the Government, which resulted in all the apartheid structures, lies at the very core of our present polarization and conflict, and to press on with it makes tragedy unavoidable. Yet, in the constitutional sphere, this is precisely what the Government appears to be doing.

I suspect that through the constitutional manipulation of the group concept, the Government hopes to share power without losing any:

'First, constitutionally and geographically identify the constituent parts, Coloured, Asian, black and white, and then let us all sit together and talk about common problems whilst avoiding each other's own affairs'. But the vast majority of people refuse to accept their constitutional identification, their geographic location and the distinction between own and general affairs. The Government underestimates the intensity of rejection, amongst blacks in particular, of this kind of constitutional tinkering. As long as Government persists, there is no way that I can see significant co-operation developing, whether on the local, regional or central level. This was brought home forcibly to me in my talk with Bishop Tutu. I differ substantially with his views on external pressure and how it can contribute to bringing about internal peace and we were discussing these differences.

Finally he said to me: 'How else can I persuade the young people not to resort to violence if I cannot focus on something which can exert non-violent pressure?'

He was quite sincere when he said this and although holes could be punched into the logic, the substantial point of the argument is far more important: 'The majority of blacks, particularly in the urban areas, do not accept or want to use the constitutional structures that the Government has created. They would rather resort to violence than be compelled to do so.' Anyone who ignores this reality in trying to bring about effective constitutional change is wasting his time.

Through its concept of the group the Government wishes to create constitutional schemes based on black, Coloured, Indian and white areas which the Government has legally prescribed.

In effect it says, 'I, the white Government, decide that as a black you must live in Soweto. Now that you are living in Soweto, it is apparent that you have your own affairs. Your own affairs do not appear to be as well off as my white own affairs, but time and budgetary formulae which I have devised will help with that. In the meantime let us see how we can get along on some general affairs. When we talk, you must realize that I am not prepared to commit myself to whether or not you are a citizen of South Africa just as I am, and whether or not you can participate on the same basis in the same constitution in the future.'

Forget about it.

The success of future constitutional negotiation will depend on our ability to restore freedom of association, including voluntary group association, and not how one party can constitutionally entrench a particular concept of the group into the constitution.

The third reason for lack of progress is confusion between decentralization of functions and devolution of autonomous powers. The Government tends to present the latter as the former. A decentralized function occurs within an overall determined framework on which the specific function has been prescribed. Instead of the central Government administering the Group Areas Act, a regional or local council can do it. The devolution of autonomous power to a regional or local body means that it has its own discretion on these and other particular issues. It is quite possible to decentralize functions whilst centralizing powers. This is precisely what the tri-cameral Parliament, getting rid of Provincial Councils and substituting them with Regional Council Services, is all about. In other words, the contentious ideological issues have been removed from the arena of bargaining and negotiation and other groups can only consult on how they snuggle into the broader scheme of things. This is the exact opposite of open-ended negotiations. For the Government to declare that it has an open agenda for constitutional negotiation, whilst continuing with the above constitutional machinations, compounds the confusion.

The above reasons are not insurmountable obstacles to effective negotiations. They can be dispensed with as a matter of choice. But that choice has to be made by those in Government and who are in charge of the negotiation process.

No looking for hidden agendas, praising Huntington or explaining away the President's slow, confusing flirtation with reform by building up the right-wing threat, can substitute for the historical responsibility that a Government in power has to initiate effective negotiation politics.

There are a number of younger Nationalist Party MPs who give me hope that this choice can be made. Even Government supporting newspapers have begun to urge quite openly that this be done. For example, in *Die Vaderland* of 26 June 1985, on the centre page, there are two articles on the significance of the Freedom Charter for blacks in particular and South African politics in general. One is by Murphy Morobe, the publicity secretary of the UDF, the other by Wynand

Malan, the Nationalist Party MP for Randburg.

The Freedom Charter was formulated on 26 June 1955, thirty years ago, as representing the views of millions of black South Africans on democracy and freedom and as their alternative to apartheid. In his article, Morobe says that the Charter: represents the views of thousands of black organizations today; is the most viable alternative to the existing constitution and makes clear that South Africa belongs to all its people. Malan, in his article, says that the Charter: 'expresses the soul of black expectations' and affirms basic human rights such as 'the right to vote' and that 'South Africa belongs to all its people'. He also agrees that 'there is much that one can identify with in the Charter, also in the white communities'. We should not romanticize such juxtapositions, but they certainly contain the seeds of a new and necessary debate.

However, the present is more sober and less inspiring when we consider the style of those who have to launch us into the politics of negotiation. I am not saying that changes or reforms are not taking place. They are and they are not unimportant. But they lack an overall sense of purpose, a declaration of intent or a satisfying response to the 'where are we going?' question. This is the choice the Government is reluctant to make and because of it, many of the benefits of reform seep away into the indifference of those who experience them, or they generate more hostility and instability. When a society goes through the transition we are experiencing, and there is no compelling and generally acceptable vision of the future that justifies the sacrifices and discomfort of the present, the problem of maintaining stability and order can become the major concern of those who govern. It is in the manner in which stability is maintained by security forces during the period of transition, that the best laid plans of mice and men can come unstuck.

Security Forces, Stability and Transition: Recently the End Conscription Campaign organized a debate with the topic: SADF: 'Shield of the Nation or Defender of Apartheid?'. Perhaps unjustifiably, I sensed that I was being set up as a punch bag for the campus trendy left in having to explain my party's position on 'delicate defence issues'. For example, I defended: the need for an able, professional defence force assisted by a volunteer reserve; that racially selective military conscription had to be phased out in bringing this about; that the Defence Force (and all security forces) had to be above political controversy as far as possible, but that it is inevitable that it will be involved in protecting also the Government of the day, pursuing its policy and that it is the task of opposition from any quarter to point out where this becomes too obvious; that any defence or security force acts pre-emptively when it wishes to prevent acts of terror or sabotage of which it has prior information; that one way of ensuring that the Defence Force can play a neutral, objective role during a period of transition is by changing its composition to a genuinely non-racial Defence Force, with no discrimination on pay, conditions of service and promotion.

For the supporters of the ECC (End Conscription Campaign) at the debate this was unimpressive stuff. The arguments against me were: the SADF is 'an instrument of the apartheid Government'; 'we are in a state of civil war' and the SADF is 'waging war against the oppressed'; compulsory military conscription is a device to 'satisfy SADF manpower needs'; to 'end conscription now' is a very important way of saying 'we will not defend apartheid'.

Two points emerged from that debate, which I believe are important. One is the misguided conception those in the ECC have of the centrality of compulsory military conscription for the Defence Force. They see this as absolutely crucial for meeting the manpower needs of the SADF. However, if the SADF dropped compulsory conscription, I believe it would relieve the moral qualms of a certain percentage of white upper-middle to middle class (predominantly English speaking) males, but would not make it impossible to recruit effectively, on a volunteer basis, from the majority of whites.

One speaker (in fact the man against me) said that an important reason why the tri-cameral Parliament was introduced was to complement the SADF manpower needs by introducing compulsory military service for Coloureds and Indians. This is poppycock. At present the SADF can cope with slightly less than half of the people coming voluntarily from those communities. This was so even before the tri-cameral Parliament came into being. If the SADF was prepared to pay competitive wages on a non-racial basis for a volunteer reserve, it would have no problem recruiting more manpower than it needs from all racial groups in the country, particularly in times of economic austerity. In terms of the logic of some of the ECC spokesmen who wish to hasten the liberation by ending conscription, they should be encouraging exactly the opposite. In other words, an extension of white male conscription for even longer periods and actively discouraging blacks, Coloureds and Asians from doing any military service at all. In this way an impossible burden will be placed on every able-bodied male and the competition between the private sector and the SADF for manpower will become increasingly unresolvable.

I do not wish to belittle the moral dilemmas raised by compulsory military conscription. They are real and I have no easy answers to them. I am responding to the *political* arguments concerning conscription and the above, concerning the centrality of conscription for SADF manpower needs, is one of them. Many of the other political arguments are old and boring; their freshness guaranteed only by the annual intake of campus cohorts who hear them for the first time. Of course, if we had the same kind of bookshops as exist in Charing Cross Road, London, then concepts such as people's army and proletarian struggle would not enjoy the status of underground literature and a lot of the deliciously daring heat around the conscription issue would die down.

For example, one thing that occupies my mind a great deal is a Defence Force as a modernizing oligarchy, suspending even the limited form of accountable Government we have now and recruiting manpower on a purely mercenary basis. What hold can a society get on such a Defence Force, except to be its coerced subjects? The picture I am painting is not an exceptional one in today's circumstances. Assad, of Syria's Alawite minority, which constitutes 11 % of the total population, governs that country with an iron fist, all in the name of modernization and reform. Here in South Africa we have not even begun to approach the level of violence and repression in Syria.

The second point that came out of the ECC debate was the degree of politicization the role of SADF had already undergone. I have raised it a number of times in debates and in discussions with the Minister and Chiefs of Staff, but I am not getting across. The attitude is usually that, because the Defence Force avoids white party political controversy 'it is above politics'. This is so off-course it is not even funny. In the same way they remain unimpressed with the arguments concerning their role in controlling unrest in the townships. Yet it is such a simplistic logic they have to counter and which they fail to do.

'Apartheid is the main cause of friction; friction leads to unrest; those who stop unrest must either take away apartheid or else defend it.'

To the extent that the role of the Police and Defence Force is becoming blurred in the minds of those who live in the townships, all Security Forces become part of the machinery to maintain control, rather than instruments to guarantee stability necessary for reform. If this distinction disappears completely so will the hope for successful reform.

I do not regard the SADF as an unthinking tool in the hands of Government, nor do I see it as a monolithic organization with a clearly defined ideology and commonly accepted collective political goals. There are differences in style, philosophy, political conviction and sense of strategic importance within its ranks. But it has a very strong chain of command and at the top of the chain are men who traffic comfortably between the military and the political executive. A General becomes an Ambassador, the chief of the Defence Force becomes Minister of Defence. Furthermore, the nature of our domestic situation is such that in regional problems, Foreign Affairs, Defence, Intelligence and Security issues overlap and reinforce each other. Somewhere a common definition of the situation is arrived at and processed for political consumption. Somewhere inputs are made into this common definition and it is eventually formulated in, I imagine, the State Security Council, before it informs the Cabinet and Parliament. One catches a glimpse of this common definition on security matters in speeches from the State President, the Minister of Defence, the Minister of Law and Order, Chief of the Defence Force, Chief of Police and sometimes even the Minister of Foreign Affairs. The language is distinctly militaristic: the enemy, onslaught, preparedness, targets, mobilization. It is the language of siege.

And so we have the extraordinary situation that two competing, perhaps contradictory, definitions of the situation are generated by the same Government. The ideology of negotiation and the ideology of siege. Both potentially refer to the same group of people. Those it wishes to negotiate with come from the same group it blames for siege. The potential fellow citizen is recruited from the same group as the potential terrorist; the responsible leader and the enemy live in the same community where unrest thrives.

And as these establishment ideologies become more clearly articulated, so the countervailing anti-establishment ideologies become clearer too. Those defined as the enemy respond by mobilizing the people's army in a war of liberation and typecast those who wish to avoid violence and seek negotiation as stooges and collaborators. At present those who choose to avoid violence and prefer negotiation are desperate to demonstrate that their strategy is of consequence. This is the point Chief Gatsha Buthelezi has repeated over and over again.

One thing is certain. If the Establishment ideology of siege and the anti-Establishment ideology of violent liberation become the main protagonists in the field of ideas in South Africa, so the moderate centre and the politics of negotiation will decline and disappear. The SADF and the security forces will play a crucial role in whether or not this is to be the case. If the response to acts of violence and sabotage is indiscriminate retaliation and tit-for-tat body-count politics, it may give short-term comfort to whites about the state of preparedness, but it will certainly not win hearts and minds in the communities where the negotiator and the liberator are competing for support. It is pointless to insist on giving some external, foreign dimension to the enemy, when his friends and relatives live in townships patrolled by Caspirs.

Does this mean that the security forces must sit on their hands in the face of a policy of deliberate sabotage and striking at so-called soft targets? Obviously not. No society, or Government for that matter, will allow the mistakes of the past, and even the plans for the future, to be wiped out by acts of terror and sabotage. But it is a commonplace of revolutionary theory that such acts are also a means to gain support amongst the very few people the Government of the day wishes to win over for its reform policies. It is also in the interaction between violence and counter-violence that the battle for the hearts and minds is being waged. In this battle the total onslaught definition of the situation is a hopeless loser.

The average young black who has to choose between believing those who wish to protect him against the total onslaught of communism or Moscow, and those who wish to liberate him from apartheid, has no problem whatsoever. The only credible alternative to the latter is a programme of liberation from apartheid, which is less costly and more plausible than a strategy of terror and violence. If the politics of negotiation cannot develop such a definition of the situation, the ideology of liberation will gain in acceptance.

In short, the actions of the security forces must be calculated to make the politics of negotiation more attractive and reasonable and not create a mood in which siege seems inevitable. Its actions must be such that those who persist with acts of violence and terror must generally appear to be unreasonable in terms of the declared goals of reform. Not unreasonable to whites, but to the very communities who are being induced to see such acts as a struggle for liberation.

My own experience of the top people in security, from the Minister of Defence and Law and Order to the Generals who give effect to their policies, is not very encouraging in the above respect. I say this without any animosity or a desire to scapegoat. These gentlemen have been extremely civil and co-operative in their attitude towards me. In any event it serves no analytical purpose to present them as demagogues and evil conspirators. Magnus Malan, the Minister of Defence, has yet to make a speech inside or outside Parliament in which he does not use a total onslaught framework; the same applies to Louis le Grange, the Minister of Law and Order. Whenever I listen to them, or their top personnel, talking in this fashion I come away with two distinct impressions. The first is, they alone know who the real enemy is and cannot really tell us about his plans. Secondly, because of this inside information, Parliament and other forms of civil Government like the media, have to be treated with a certain degree of strategic disrespect.

I very seldom come away from a briefing, or a security debate, without feeling manipulated. Nothing brought it home stronger this year than the Minister of Foreign Affairs' contemptuous statement in Parliament that the Government had been supporting RENAMO prior to Nkomati and would do so again if necessary. This, after we had probed, without success, to get a confirmation about it two years earlier.

This kind of experience leads me to the conclusion that if the ideology of siege and onslaught is the prevailing one in Government, then the security forces must work according to an agenda and timetable of which only their leadership has any knowledge and which functions independently of any agenda to actively and publicly promote the politics of negotiation. It is far easier to persuade whites about the validity of siege than it is to convince blacks about the credibility of negotiation.

I began by saying that at the end of '85 session of the tri-cameral Parliament, the only thing that was clear was the confusion. The above impressions about the leading personalities, events, departments and organizations shaped my conclusion. I also began by saying that I still believed a way could be found to avoid confrontation and promote negotiation.

Is this just whistling in the dark? No, I do not think so. The reason for optimism rather than outright despair lies in the fact that if all the major interest groups in society were to be arranged on a continuum from preserving the status quo to changing it, the vast majority of them would be on the side of changing it. If this axis is intersected with a violent/non-violent continuum, the vast majority would still fall within the less violent strategies for change.

When I talk about interest groups, I include sections of Government, the Civil Service, the Press, business, labour, political and quasi-political organizations, church and cultural movements. I am convinced that significant sections of those movements who have committed themselves to violent strategies could still be persuaded otherwise.

But the Joker in the pack is Government. If it calls siege it will be siege; if it calls both siege and negotiation it will be siege in any case. There may come a time when the option of calling anything will have passed it by, but that time is not yet.

What kind of checklist of steps would make a significant contribution towards promoting the politics of negotiation and undercutting the impact of strategies of violence? I think the following:

1. Fundamentally change the attitude of the security forces towards legitimate dissent and the control of unrest in the townships.
2. Increase the size and facilities of the ordinary police force to cope with normal crime prevention.
3. Limit the operations of riot police to clearly defined exceptional circumstances and ensure that they have all the necessary equipment for conventional riot control.
4. Get rid of a total onslaught approach towards both external and

internal opposition to Government policy. In particular, separate the SADF from police functions.
5. Suspend all constitutional tinkering until a commonly accepted Declaration of Intent has been worked out.
6. State unequivocably that influx control is going to be scrapped completely.
7. Declare that one constitution, based on one citizenship without entrenched racial domination, will have to be negotiated for all population groups.
8. Release Nelson Mandela and other political prisoners unconditionally and make it clear that they can take the above message to their respective organizations.
9. Commit the Government to the restoration of freedom of association in social, economic and political activities in South Africa, including group membership. At the same time make it quite clear that subversion and violence will not go unpunished.
10. Encourage the media, TV, Radio and Press, to promote the above points in order to create a climate conducive to the politics of negotiation.

The least that such steps will achieve, will be to make strategies of violence and terror appear more unreasonable and reduce the all or nothing appeal of an ideology of liberation. At the same time it will force Government to choose clearly for the ideology of negotiation rather than siege. At most, it will draw some heavyweight customers into the workshop of reform. Without them no negotiation can succeed.

Will we make it? This must be the most overworked question on the South African condition. I call it and similar ones God-questions, because only Providence has the omniscience to answer.

My response to this question was captured perfectly this year when Jeremy and I were dragging our undertrained, aching bodies past the halfway mark in the Peninsula Marathon. A woozy-boozy, raggedy clad figure, with an Andy Capp cap on his head, jumped from the crowd in front of us.

Shaking the wrists and fingers of both hands in our faces and smiling at us with unfocused eyes he shouted, 'Your problem is time man; your problem is time'.

We just made it. That is it, a combination of time and effort. The more you give of one, the less you are in need of the other.

On 20 July 1985, the State President declared a State of Emergency in thirty-six magisterial districts.